BTH / N / VI - R

W9-BSB-738

NEVER BE
LIED TO
AGAIN

BY THE SAME AUTHOR

Instant Analysis

NEVER BE LIED TO AGAIN

HOW TO GET THE TRUTH
IN 5 MINUTES OR LESS
IN ANY CONVERSATION OR SITUATION

DAVID J. LIEBERMAN, PH.D.

ST. MARTIN'S PRESS

NEW YORK

Production Editor: David Stanford Burr
Design: Chris Welch

Library of Congress Cataloging-in-Publication Data

Lieberman, David J.
    Never be lied to again : how to get the truth in 5 minutes or less
in any conversation or situation / David J. Lieberman. — 1st ed.
        p.   cm.
    ISBN 0-312-18634-7 (hardcover)
    1. Truthfulness and falsehood.   2. Deception.   I. Title.
BF637.T77L54   1998
158.2—dc21   98-18634
                                                                    CIP

First Edition: July 1998

10   9   8   7   6

CONTENTS

CONTENTS

CONTENTS

PART III. TACTICS FOR DETECTING DECEIT AND GATHERING INFORMATION IN CASUAL CONVERSATIONS

PART IV. MIND GAMES

PART V. ADVANCED TECHNIQUES

PART VI.
PSYCHOLOGY ON YOUR SIDE

PART VII. INTERNAL TRUTH BLOCKERS: WE LIE LOUDEST WHEN WE LIE TO OURSELVES

PART VIII. EXTERNAL TRUTH BLOCKERS: TRICKS OF THE TRADE

CONTENTS

ACKNOWLEDGMENTS

I would like to thank Jennifer Enderlin, my editor at St. Martin's. She is an exceptional talent whose ability is matched only by her boundless passion for her work.

And to those who have worked tirelessly, my warmest thanks to the publicity, marketing, advertising, and sales departments at St. Martin's for their intense efforts and commitment: Alison Lazarus, John Cunningham, Steve Kasdin, John Murphy, Jamie Brickhouse, Mike Storrings, Janet Wagner, Mark Kohut, and James Wehrle, and to the entire Broadway Sales Department for their continued efforts on behalf of this book. A special thanks to St. Martin's publisher, Sally Richardson, for her vast enthusiasm and belief in this project.

A thousand thanks to David Stanford Burr, production editor, and Nancy Inglis, copy editor, for their outstanding work on the manuscript. Their hard work and diligence is evident throughout this entire book.

I would like to thank my agents, Michael Larsen and Elizabeth Pomada. The success of their agency is a clear reflection of their professionalism and dedication. In an industry of giants, they stand without equals.

My infinite appreciation and gratitude to Barbara and William O'Rourke, who gave me the two things every writer needs: tranquility and computer help. And my thanks to Laurie Rosin, one of the nation's leading freelance editors, for invaluable input and suggestions.

While much of information in this book is based on newly developed and leading-edge research and technologies, I would be remiss if I did not acknowledge the evolution of the process and contributions of those giants in the fields of human behavior, linguistics, and hypnosis: Milton Erickson, Robert Cialdini, Paul Ekman, Elliot Aronson, Judson Mills, Stephen Worchel, Jack Brehm, Stanley Milgram, and Ray Birdwhistell.

A NOTE TO READERS

To those in law enforcement: make sure that you check appropriate federal and state laws regarding both interviewing and interrogation. Those in the private sector must use judgment and common sense when using this system. Caution is always advised when you are dealing with individuals suspected of illegal acts or illicit activities.

There will be those who will try to use this information to manipulate others and exploit situations. But do you hold back information that can help people because of a fear that there will be those who will abuse it? To live in a world where information is distributed based upon the damage that can be caused by the lowest common denominator is to spiral away from progress and away from hope.

It is with high hope and expectation that the techniques in this book will be used appropriately, with benevolence, and with the purposes for which they were intended.

INTRODUCTION

THE PROCESS AND THE POWER

Honesty is at the cornerstone of every relationship, whether it's business or personal. Being aware of someone else's true intentions is undeniably valuable, often saving you time, money, energy, and heartache. When you know a person's true intent, you have the power to control the situation, or at the very least not be taken advantage of.

There is no greater ability than consistently and constantly making the right decisions in life. Remember, though, your decisions are only as solid and right as the facts that you base them on. You will learn how to get at the message beneath the words, how to know what people are thinking when they don't say what's really on their mind. A former client of mine put it best when she said, "It's like having a man inside their camp—an outpost in their head."

In an ideal society there would be no need for lies or for this book. But we live in a world of deception. And whether you want to play or not, you're in the game. The question is, do you want to win? In romance you need never play the fool again. In business you'll get the upper hand. Wherever and whenever you deal with people, you'll have the tools to come out a winner.

WHAT'S IN THIS BOOK AND HOW TO USE IT

I'm what is affectionately referred to as a hired gun, a specialist in the field of human behavior. As a board-certified hypnotherapist with a Ph.D. in psychology, I represent corporations as well as private individuals, and offer a type of leverage that many high-paid attorneys, top-notch accountants, and seasoned executives cannot.

Too often we miss the meaning behind the message. As you know, people don't always say what they mean or mean what they say. This book focuses on the truth and how to get at it.

To be an effective negotiator, you must use many strategies and techniques, all of them relying upon the accuracy of the information you're given. The answers you get from the world's most powerful supercomputer are worthless if the numbers you give it to work with are wrong.

We often forget how easily facts can get lost in a conversation, negotiation, or interrogation. Abraham Lincoln is said to have posed the following question: "How many legs would a sheep have if you called its tail a leg?" "Four," explained Lincoln. "Because calling its tail a leg doesn't make it one."

While people lie for many different reasons, their lying rarely benefits the person lied to. And there's that one undeniable truth about lying. Everybody does it, but nobody likes it when it's done to them.

It takes at least two people for a lie to be effective—one to offer the lie and one to believe it. And while we certainly can't stop people from trying to lie to us, we can keep them from being successful.

This book is divided into eight parts, each of which explores a facet of lying. The innovative techniques in this book will help you figure out if you're being lied to. If you are the victim of a deception, they will assist you in getting at the truth and in gaining control over the situation. Many of the examples in this book are drawn from personal relationships and business situations; certainly most of us can identify with these scenarios.

PART 1

SIGNS OF DECEPTION

This book picks up where others leave off, going well beyond observing body language clues. The first part offers a catalog of forty-six clues to deception, divided into seven sections. Some of the clues involve the fundamentals of body language, while others use more advanced techniques and processes such as psycholinguistic emphasis and neural linguistic choice perception. Each section concludes with a summary for easy reference.

PART 2

BECOMING A HUMAN LIE DETECTOR

"We often fly blind into verbal combat." That is to say, we usually think of the questions we *should* have asked two days after the battle is over. This section offers a specific game plan to detect deceit, detailing exactly what to say and when to say it. This sophisticated system involves choosing from a variety of scripted sequences, each from a different psychological angle. Each script includes a primer, an attack sequence, and silver bullets.

PART 3

TACTICS FOR DETECTING DECEIT AND GATHERING INFORMATION IN CASUAL CONVERSATIONS

Now what about those times in casual conversation when you think someone might be lying to you, but a full-fledged interrogation is out of the question? This section provides phenomenal techniques for gathering more information without being obvious. You will also learn how to steer a conversation in any direction that you choose in order to get the information that you want. This section also covers those times when different tactics are necessary for getting to the truth, instances where you may not have the leverage you need. The psychological process is different than if you were coming from a position of strength.

PART 4

MIND GAMES

"Mind Games" includes two simple techniques that provide extraordinary results. When you use the first, almost no one will be able to lie to you. When you employ the second, you will be able to discern anybody's true intentions and motivation in any situation.

PART 5

ADVANCED TECHNIQUES

This section presents the most advanced and groundbreaking techniques for getting at the truth. Using a blend of hypnosis and a system I have developed called Trance-Scripts, you'll be able to give commands directly to people's unconscious minds—all in conversation and without their awareness. Through this process you can persuade others to tell the truth.

PART 6

PSYCHOLOGY ON YOUR SIDE

This part explores the ten fundamental laws of human behavior, the principles that govern our thinking. Once you
learn these laws, you'll know how to get the truth out of
anyone. With an understanding of how the brain processes
information, you will be able to easily influence other people's decisions.

PART 7

INTERNAL TRUTH BLOCKERS

Here's the biggest truth in a book about lying: we lie loudest
when we lie to ourselves. We all know someone who absolutely refuses to believe that his or her spouse is unfaithful,
despite all the warning signs. This section shows you how
to become aware of and eliminate those internal blockers
that keep you from seeing what's really going on.

PART 8

EXTERNAL TRUTH BLOCKERS

This section lets us in on the psychological secrets of the experts. You will discover how the pros—from professional poker players to master negotiators—keep you from perceiving the facts in an objective fashion, even affect your ability to evaluate information. The influence of the pros is enormous; they can have a powerful impact on your perception of reality—unless, of course, you've read this book and can outthink them.

Note to readers: Throughout all of the examples in this book the pronouns *he* and *she* are used alternately. This was done to make the language less sexist, not to indicate that one sex is more likely to lie in given situations than the other.

PART

1

SIGNS OF DECEPTION

"He that has eyes to see and ears to hear may convince himself that no mortal can keep a secret. If his lips are silent, he chatters with his fingertips; betrayal oozes out of him at every pore."

—SIGMUND FREUD

This part contains a catalog of forty-six clues to deception, divided into seven sections. The clues can be used independently or in conjunction with one another. While some are excellent indicators by themselves, all clues should be viewed within the context of the situation at hand; they are not absolutes.

Some of these are so subtle that they can easily be missed unless you pay close attention. Others may be glaringly obvious. In some instances you'll be looking for lies of omission—what's missing that should be there. Other times you'll be dealing with lies of commission—things said or done that are inconsistent with the rest of the message.

Occasionally you won't have access to all these clues: you might be on the telephone, for instance, and not be able to see the body of the person you are talking to. It's not necessary to memorize these clues, for in time they will become second nature: you will gradually become more familiar with what to look for, what to listen for, and what to ask for, to get to the truth.

Certain variables such as gender, ethnicity, and cultural background can influence how we interpret various clues—the use of gestures and personal space, for example. For the most part, though, these factors are negligable and can be ignored.

Some of the clues draw on traditional psychological disciplines such as body language and psycholinguistics. These are used to detect discrepancies between the verbal and the nonverbal message. You will also be using more sophisticated methods developed as a result of my research in the field of human behavior. One such tool, psycholinguistic emphasis (PLE), involves the words that people choose to reflect their current psychological state.

Once you realize that you're being lied to, should you confront the liar immediately? Usually not. The best approach is to note the fact in your mind and continue with the conversation, trying to extract more information. Once you confront someone who has lied to you, the tone of the conversation changes and gathering additional facts becomes difficult. Therefore, wait until you have all the evidence you want and then decide whether to confront the person at that time or hold off to figure how you can best use this insight to your advantage.

SECTION 1

BODY LANGUAGE

Our fingers, hands, arms, and legs and their movements offer a fascinating insight into our true feelings. Most people aren't aware that their body speaks a language all its own; try as they will to deceive you with their words, the truth can be always silently observed.

You may already have read or heard about some of these clues, but they are only a small portion of the tactics that you will learn.

The Language of the Eyes

No or little direct eye contact is a classic sign of deception. A person who is lying to you will do everything to avoid making eye contact. Unconsciously he feels you will be able to see through him—via his eyes. And feeling guilty, he doesn't want to face you. Instead he will glance down or his eyes may dart from side to side. Conversely, when we tell the truth or we're offended by a false accusation, we tend to give our full focus and have fixed concentration. We lock eyes with our accuser as if to say "You're not getting away until we get to the bottom of this."

The Body Never Lies

Lacking Animation

The hands and arms are excellent indicators of deceit because they are used to gesture with and are more easily visible than our feet and legs. But hands, arms, legs, and feet can *all* give us information if we're watching carefully. When someone is lying or keeping something in, he tends to be less expressive with his hands or arms. He may keep them on his lap if he's sitting, or at his side if he's standing; he may stuff his hands in his pockets or clench them. Fingers may be folded into the hands; full extension of the fingers is usually a gesture of openness.

Have you ever noticed that when you're passionate about what you're saying, your hands and arms wave all about, emphasizing your point and conveying your enthusiasm? And have you ever realized that when you don't believe in what you're saying, your body language echoes these feelings and becomes inexpressive?

Additionally, if you ask someone a question and her hands clench or go palm down, this is a sign of defensiveness and withdrawal. If she is genuinely confused at the accusations or the line of questioning, her hands turn palm-up as if to say "Give me more information; I do not understand" or "I have nothing to hide."

Keeping Something In

When a person sits with his legs and arms close to his body, perhaps crossed but not outstretched, he is evincing the thought *I'm keeping something in*. His arms and legs may be crossed because he feels he must defend himself. When we feel comfortable and confident we tend to stretch out—claim our space, as it were. When we feel less secure, we take up less physical space and fold our arms and legs into our body, into what is almost a fetal position.

Displaying Artificial Movements

Arm movements and gestures seem stiff and almost mechanical. This behavior can be readily observed by watching unpolished actors and politicians. They try to use gestures to convince us that they're impassioned about their beliefs, but there's no fluidity to their movements. The movements are contrived, not natural.

The Unconscious Cover-up

If her hand goes straight to her face while she is responding to a question or when she is making a statement, this is often an indication of deceit. Her hand may cover her mouth while she is speaking, indicating that she really doesn't believe what she is saying to be true; it acts as a screen, an unconscious attempt to hide her words.

When she is listening she covers or touches her face as an unconscious manifestation of the thought *I really don't want to be listening to this*. Touching the nose is also considered to be a sign of deception, as well as scratching behind or on the side of the ear or rubbing the eyes.

This should not be confused with the posture associated with deep thought, which usually conveys concentration and attention.

CLUE 4

The Partial Shrug

The shrugging of one's shoulders is a gesture that usually indicates ignorance or indifference: "I don't know" or "I don't care." If a person makes this gesture he or she usually means to communicate that very message. However, if this gesture is fleeting—if you catch only a glimpse of it—it's a sign of something else. This person is trying to demonstrate that she is casual and relaxed about her answer, when in fact she really isn't. Because what she feels isn't a true emotion, she doesn't really shrug.

This situation is similar to that of someone who is embarrassed by a joke but wants to pretend that she thinks it's funny. What you see is a "lips only" smile, not a big grin encompassing her entire face.

SUMMARY

- The person will make little or no eye contact.
- Physical expression will be limited, with few arm and hand movements. What arm and hand movements are present will seem stiff, and mechanical. Hands, arms, and legs pull in toward the body; the individual takes up less space.
- His hand(s) may go up to his face or throat. But contact with his body is limited to these areas. He is also unlikely to touch his chest with an open hand gesture.

- If he is trying to appear casual and relaxed about his answer, he may shrug a little.

EMOTIONAL STATES: CONSISTENCY AND CONTRADICTION

Individual gestures need to be looked at by themselves *and* in relation to what is being said. In this section we're going to look at the relationship between words and the corresponding gestures. Besides obvious inconsistencies such as shaking your head from side to side while saying yes, more subtle but equally revealing signs of deception exist. These take place at both the conscious and the unconscious level.

Then there are times when we make a conscious effort to emphasize our point, but because the gesture is forced it lacks spontaneity and the timing is off. When you know what to look for, this is readily apparent.

Inconsistencies between gestures, words, and *emotions* are also great indicators, in that you're presented with a dual message. One example is a person who grins while she expresses sorrow to a friend whose spouse has left her.

Watch for what is known as the initial reaction expression (IRE). This is an initial expression of true feelings that may last for less than a second, just until the person you are observing has a chance to mask them. Even if you can't read the fleeting expression, the fact that it has changed is reason enough to suspect that the emotion you are currently seeing is false.

Timing Is Everything

If the person's head begins to shake in a confirming direction before or as the words come out, this is a good indication that he is telling the truth. However, if he shakes his head *after* the point is made, he may be trying to demonstrate conviction, but because it's a contrived movement—one not based on emotion—the timing is off.

Also look for hand and arm movements that punctuate a point *after* it's been made. The gesture looks like an afterthought because that's what it is. He wants to get his words out fast but realizes that maybe he should *look* really mad and play the part. Additionally, hand and arm movements will not only start late but will seem mechanical and won't coincide with verbal punctuation.

If you wanted to convince someone that you were angry when you really weren't, you would want to play the part and look angry. But there's more to it than that. The timing of that angry facial expression matters. If the facial expression comes *after* the verbal statement ("I am so angry with you right now" . . . pause . . . and then the angry expression), it looks false. Showing the expression *before* the "I'm so angry" line wouldn't indicate deceptiveness. It would only suggest that you are thinking about what you are saying or are having some difficulty in deciding how to express your anger.

Also, someone who believes in his words will be inclined to move his head on important syllables to drive home a point. Whether up and down or side to side, the head movement is supposed to punctuate particular points and ideas. A mechanical nodding without regard to emphasis indicates a conscious movement. These conscious movements are intended to show emphasis, but when a person is lying such movements are not part of the natural rhythm of the message.

CLUE 6

Contradiction and Consistency

Not only is the timing important, but we need to pay attention to the *type* of gesture. The woman who frowns as she says she loves you is sending a contradictory message. An obvious incongruence between gestures and speech indicates that the speaker is lying. A good example is the man who tries to tell his girlfriend he loves her while shaking his fist in the air. Similarly, hands tightly clenched and a statement of pleasure are not in synch with each other. Make sure that the gesture fits the speech.

CLUE 7

The Emotion Commotion

The timing of emotions is something that's difficult to fake. Watch closely and you probably won't be fooled. A response that's not genuine is not spontaneous; therefore, there is a slight delay in the onset of false emotion. The duration of the emotion is also off: The response goes on longer than it would in the case of genuine emotion. The fade-out—how the emotion ends—is abrupt. So the emotion is delayed coming on, stays longer than it should, and fades out abruptly.

The emotion of surprise is a great example. Surprise comes and goes quickly, so if it is prolonged it is most likely false. But when we are feigning surprise, most of us keep a look of awe plastered on our faces; this look won't really fool an aware observer.

CLUE 8

The Expression Zone: Beware the Smile That Doesn't Seem Happy

Deception expressions are often confined to the mouth area. A smile that's genuine lights up the whole face. When a smile is forced, the person's mouth is closed and tight and there's no movement in the eyes or forehead. A smile that does not involve the whole face is a sign of deception.

While we're on this subject, be aware that the smile is the

most common mask for emotion because it best conceals the appearance in the lower face of anger, disgust, sadness, or fear. In other words, a person who doesn't want her true feelings to be revealed may "put on a happy face." But remember, if the smile does not reflect a true emotion—happiness, for example—it will not encompass her entire face.

SUMMARY

- The timing is off between gestures and words.
- The head moves in a mechanical fashion.
- Gestures don't match the verbal message.
- The timing and duration of emotional gestures will seem off.
- Expression will be limited to the mouth area when the person is feigning certain emotions—happiness, surprise, awe, and so on.

SECTION 3

INTERPERSONAL INTERACTIONS

You want to be aware of a person's posture in and of itself *and* in relation to his surroundings. How the person carries himself and behaves in relation to what he says is an excellent indication of his comfort level.

It's widely believed that when we are wrongfully accused

we become defensive. In fact, generally speaking, only a guilty person gets defensive. Someone who is innocent will usually go on the offensive. If Mary and John are arguing and Mary accuses John of something, John doesn't automatically assume a defensive posture. If he is innocent and objects to what Mary is saying, he will go on the offensive. The following clues look at the distinctions between these two states of mind.

CLUE 9

The Head Shift

If someone is uttering or listening to a message that makes her uncomfortable, her head may shift away from the one she is talking to. This is an attempt to distance herself from the source of the discomfort. If she is comfortable with her position and secure in her actions, she will move her head toward the other person in an attempt to get closer to the source of information. Watch for an immediate and pronounced jerking of the head or a slow deliberate withdrawal. Either may happen.

This action is very different from—and should not be confused with—a slight *tilt* of the head to the side. This occurs when we hear something of interest. It's considered to be a vulnerable pose and would not be adopted by a person with something to hide.

CLUE 10

The Posture of a Liar

When a person feels confident about a situation and conversation, he stands erect or sits up straight. This behavior also indicates how people feel about themselves in general. Those who are secure and confident stand tall, with shoulders back. Those who are insecure or unsure of themselves often stand hunched over, with their hands in their pockets.

Studies have shown that the best way to avoid being mugged is to walk briskly, with your head up and your arms moving. Such a style of moving conveys confidence. A conversation that produces feelings of confidence or those of insecurity will produce the concomitant physical posture.

CLUE 11

If She's Headed for the Door . . .

Just as we move away from someone who threatens us physically, the person who feels at a psychological disadvantage will shift or move away from her accuser. When we feel passionate about our ideas, in an attempt to persuade the other person, we move toward him. The liar is reluctant to move toward or even face the source of the threat. She turns sideways or completely away and rarely stands squared off. The face-to-face demeanor is reserved for the person who seeks to refute a slanderous statement. This is not the case when there's deceit.

Also look for a movement in the direction of the exit. Feeling uncomfortable, she may angle her body or actually move toward the exit. While standing she may position her back to the wall. Her psychological exposure causes her to seek physical refuge. Feeling verbally ambushed, she wants to make sure that she can see what's coming next. Those who are confident and comfortable don't mind taking center stage.

If He's Not Touchin', He's Probably Bluffin'

The person who is being deceitful will have little or no physical contact with the one he is talking to. This is an excellent and quite reliable indicator. While making a false statement, or during a conversation containing one, the liar will rarely touch the other person. He's unconsciously reducing the level of intimacy to help alleviate his guilt. Touch indicates psychological connection; it's used when we believe strongly in what we're saying.

The Finger That Never Points

Someone who is lying or hiding something rarely points a finger, either at others or straight up in the air. Finger pointing indicates conviction and authority as well as emphasis of a point. Someone who's not standing on solid ground probably won't be able to muster this nonverbal cue of disdain.

Roadblocks, Barriers, and Obstacles

See if he uses inanimate objects—a pillow, a drinking glass, anything—to form a barrier between you and him. Just as you would shield yourself from physical harm, so, too, does he protect himself from a verbal assault. How comfortable someone is with a particular topic can be readily seen in how open he is to discussing it. Placing a physical barrier between you and him is the verbal equivalent of "I don't want to talk about it," indicating deception or a covert intention. Since he can't get up and leave, his displeasure manifests itself in the formation of physical barriers between him and the source of the discomfort.

Jim, a colleague of mine, told me an interesting story about his former boss, who was president of a large manufacturing company. Whenever Jim was in the boss's office and brought up employee problems, product flaws, or anything that made the president uncomfortable, his boss would place his coffee mug on the desk in front of him, between them both. Then he would casually and quite unconsciously line up all of the desk accessories, forming a clear barrier between himself and his employee.

SUMMARY

- There's movement away from his accuser, possibly in the direction of the exit.
- He is reluctant to face his accuser and may turn his head or shift his body away.
- The person who is lying will probably slouch; he is unlikely to stand tall with his arms out or outstretched.
- There will be little or no physical contact during his attempt to convince you.
- He will not point his finger at the person he is trying to convince.
- He may place physical objects between himself and his accuser.

SECTION 4

WHAT IS SAID: ACTUAL VERBAL CONTENT

"The cruelest lies are often told in silence."
—ROBERT LOUIS STEVENSON

The words we choose to express ourselves provide a window to our true feelings. When we wish to deceive, we choose certain words, phrases, and syntax that we *think* will convey truth in our message. Think of the many ways you can communicate the word *yes*, from the verbal to the nonverbal.

How we choose to express ourselves indicates how strongly we believe what we say.

There are subtle differences between what the truth sounds like and what a lie dressed up to sound truthful sounds like. The words we choose to convey a message are much more reflective of our true feelings than you might suspect.

Using Your Words to Make His Point

Have you ever noticed how you respond to social gestures of courtesy when you're preoccupied? In the morning, when you walk into your office and someone says "Good morning" to you, you respond with "Good morning." If you're greeted with "Hello," you answer "Hello." You're just not interested in making the effort to think.

In this clue, though, the person accused doesn't have *time* to think, so he reflects back the statement of his accuser out of fear. Because he is caught off guard, he replies using the other person's words, but in the negative. Making a positive statement negative is the fastest way to get the words out. For example, an aggrieved spouse asks, "Did you cheat on me?" The liar answers, "No, I didn't cheat on you." "Did you ever cheat on me?" draws the response "No, I never cheated on you." *Did* you becomes *didn't* and *ever* becomes *never*. Remember, above all else, the guilty wants to get his answer out fast. Any delay makes him feel like he appears more guilty. And to the guilty every second that passes seems like an eternity.

Skilled interviewers and interrogators know the following rule concerning contractions. When a suspect uses a contraction—"It *wasn't* me" instead of "It *was not* me"—statistically speaking, there is a 60 percent chance he's being truthful. Sometimes the guilty, in an attempt to sound emphatic, don't want to use a contraction in their statement of innocence; they want to emphasize the *not*.

CLUE 16

The More He Tries, the More You Should Worry

It's often been said that the best people to sell to are those who have signs posted saying NO SALESMAN OR SOLICITORS. These people know that they can be sold anything, so they attempt to deflect salespeople from trying.

A person speaking the truth is not concerned about whether you misunderstand him; he is always willing to clarify. The liar wants to be sure that you understand his point immediately so that he can change the subject and no further questions will be asked. When his evidence is fragile, the words he uses are bold and solid, to compensate. For example, asked if he ever cheated on a test in law school, Peter might respond with "I'm pretty sure I never did." If he had and wanted to convince someone to the contrary, his response is likely to be more definitive: "No, I would never cheat on a test." Of course someone who never has cheated might give the same answer, so this statement needs to be considered in the context of the conversation and in conjunction with other clues.

Sometimes people who adamantly assert an opinion or view don't even hold it themselves. If they were confident in their thinking, they would not feel a need to compensate. If someone says right up front that he positively won't budge, it means one thing: He knows he can be swayed. He needs to tell you this so you won't ask, because he know he'll cave in.

Ironically, the confident person will use phrases like "I'm sorry, this is pretty much the best we can do" or "I'm afraid there's not a whole lot of room for negotiation here." This person's words provide comfort for his opponent, not a shield for himself.

The Good Old Freudian Slip

Sometimes we say one thing when we mean to say another. This is referred to as a Freudian slip, a subconscious leak when a person's misspoken words reflect and reveal his true feelings, thoughts, or intentions. For example, someone who means to say, "We worked really hard on the project; it took us all night to *complete* it," might slip and say, "We worked really hard on the project; it took us all night to *copy* it."

There's a great joke about these unconscious slip-ups. A

man confessed to his friend that he had made a Freudian slip during a recent dinner with his parents. He said, "I meant to say 'Could you please pass the salt?' to my mother. Instead it came out as 'I had a terrible childhood and you've ruined my life, you wicked woman.' "

CLUE 18

I'm Above That Sort of Thing

When a person is asked a question, if he responds with an answer that depersonalizes and globalizes the question, be aware. Let's say you ask someone, "Were you honest with me about our conversation yesterday?" Watch out if you get a reply like "Of course I was. I would never lie to you. You know how I feel about lying." Or when someone is asked, "Did you ever steal from your last job?" he responds with, "No, I think stealing from one's job is the worst thing you can do." Or "Did you ever cheat on me?" And you hear, "You know I'm against that sort of thing. I think it morally reprehensible." To sound more emphatic, a liar offers abstract assurances as evidence of his innocence in a specific instance. In his mind the evidence doesn't weigh favorably for him, so he brings in his fictitious belief system to back him up.

Silence Is Gold-Plated

Have you ever experienced a first date where a lapse in conversation caused uneasiness or anxiety? When you're
uncomfortable, silence adds to your discomfort. Conversely,
some married couples can be comfortable in each other's
presence for hours without a single word being exchanged.
The guilty are uncomfortable with silence.

When someone is asked a question, take notice if he continues to add more information without being prodded. A
typical scenario would go like this: You ask Jack where he
was Friday night. He responds with "I was out with my
friends." You don't acknowledge his answer. Jack gets nervous because in his mind he hasn't sold you. So he goes on:
"We went to the movies." He'll continue adding new facts
until you respond, thus letting him know that he's convinced
you.

This should not be confused with the person who says it
all right away. The guilty tells his story in dribs and drabs
until he gets a verbal confirmation to stop. He speaks to fill
the gap left by the silence.

An Implied Answer Is No Answer

Often when a person doesn't want to respond to a question
he will imply an answer. For example, Ralph is speaking on

the telephone with a girl he has never met before. He says jokingly, "So, are you gorgeous?" She proceeds to tell him that she works out three times a week, takes an aerobics class every other day, and has dated several male models. This is a nonanswer. She is attempting to circumvent the question altogether by *implying* that she is attractive.

The following exchange is from a press conference between reporter Helen Thomas and President Nixon's press secretary, Ronald Ziegler, during the Watergate scandal.

THOMAS: Has the President asked for any resignations so far and have any been submitted or on his desk?
ZIEGLER: I have repeatedly stated, Helen, that there is no change in the status of the White House staff.
THOMAS: But that was not the question. Has he asked for any resignations?
ZIEGLER: I understand the question, and I heard it the first time. Let me go through my answer. As I have said, there is no change in the status of the White House staff. There have been no resignations submitted.

The question "Has the President asked for any resignations?" was not answered either directly or indirectly. Ziegler tried to *imply* that he was giving an answer to the question, but he never did answer it.

SUMMARY

- He will use your words to make his point.
- He will keep adding more information until he's sure that he has sold you on his story.
- He may stonewall, giving the impression that his mind is made up. This is often an attempt to limit your challenges to his position.
- Watch out for the good old Freudian slip.
- He depersonalizes his answer by offering his belief on the subject instead of answering directly.
- He may imply an answer but never state it directly.

SECTION 5

HOW SOMETHING IS SAID

"What is the use of lying when the truth, well distributed, serves the same purpose."
—W.E. FORSTER

I know a hair stylist who would go into the woman's purse for his tip after the haircut. No one ever got upset with him because he did it in such an innocent way that you just had to laugh. It's how he did it that made all the difference.

Two salespeople can read all the manuals on selling and learn all the sales pitches there are, and one will still sell far more than the other. While the two speak the same words, these words convey completely different messages. How something is said is often just as important as what is said.

Emphasis on different parts of a sentence can covey completely different meanings. Notice the different ways the phrase "Michelle was caught stealing from her boss" can be interpreted depending upon where the emphasis is placed.

Michelle / was / caught / stealing / from her / boss
    a   b   c   d   e   f

a. By emphasizing the name *Michelle*, you're conveying the significance of who stole.
b. Emphasis on *was* draws attention to the fact that it has already happened.
c. Emphasis on *caught* indicates that the fact that she got caught is unusual.
d. Stress on *stealing* lets us know that stealing is out of character for her.
e. If *from her* is emphasized, the fact that she stole from her own boss is unusual.
f. Emphasis on *boss* shows that it was unusual for her to steal from a boss—any boss.

This section explores the subtleties of communication. You will see how the speaker's hidden thoughts are always hinged to the expression of his words.

CLUE 21

Speedy Gonzales

There's a rule of thumb about the speed at which an individual answers. It is most germane when you ask about intangibles—attitudes or beliefs—instead of facts. A well known restaurant chain uses a timed test response in their hiring process. They will ask the interviewee if she has any prejudices against other ethnic groups or if she feels uncomfortable working with or serving certain people. The longer it takes her to answer no, the lower her score. This question concerns a belief and requires internal processing. Someone who holds no such prejudice answers quickly. A person who is prejudiced takes longer to evaluate the question and formulate her answer. The prejudiced person tries to come up with the "right" answer, which takes more time than merely giving an honest answer.

Another element to consider is pacing. How fast does the rest of the sentence follow the initial one-word response? In truthful statements a fast no or yes is followed quickly by an explanation. If the person is being deceitful the rest of the sentence may come more slowly because she gets that no or yes out quickly but then needs time to think up an explanation.

Compensation

Be suspicious of someone whose reaction is all out of proportion to the question or comment. This person is attempting to accomplish a variety of objectives. She wants to appear outraged by the accusation, but she is not. So she exaggerates her displeasure, often ending up going a little overboard. She tries to convince you because the evidence doesn't. As Shakespeare said, "The lady doth protest too much." Also beware of diatribes where she repeats points that she has already made.

Sometimes a person may claim to be indignant about a cause or belief because he is trying to convince himself along with his accuser. This reaction, interestingly enough, takes place at the unconscious level. The man who claims to be adamantly against prostitution may be covering up his true feelings, which are the exact opposite. Not wanting to become consciously aware of what he really believes, he reinforces his overt attitude by expressing it aggressively. Of course, though, the person could just be passionate about his cause, so this statement needs to be viewed within the context of the conversation.

This person is also reluctant to use words that convey attachment and ownership. For example, while lying about his car having been stolen, he may refer to it as "the car" or "that car" and not "my car" or "our car." When lying about a relationship or actions toward a person, he may use such phrases as "that child," or "the relationship," instead of "my child" or "our relationship."

Emphasis Makes the Meaning

The pronouns *I*, *we*, and *us* are underused or absent. The liar doesn't want to own his words. When a person is making a truthful statement, he emphasizes the pronoun as much as or more than the rest of the sentence. Instead of saying, "Yes, I am," a person who is lying may respond with a simple yes.

Words of expression are not emphasized. For example, "We had a *greeeat* time!" conveys ownership of his words. Now say quickly, "It went great"—bland and noncommittal.

When a person is speaking truthfully, the initial one-or two-word agreement or denial may be elongated for emphasis—"Nooo," "Yeeesss," or "Of courrrse." This type of emphasis is usually absent in deception. This elongation occurs because the person is comfortable with his position and doesn't mind "playing" with his answer. A friend of mine who is an acting coach tells me that unpolished actors often speak all the words in their lines with equal emphasis, a dead giveaway that they are novices. The simple practice of elongating key words often makes for much more believable performances.

Additionally, there will probably be no highs or lows, just in-betweens. Not only is the voice higher—like any other muscle, the vocal cords tighten under stress—but varied voice inflection may be missing. We generally use inflection for emphasis when we are making a point. A deceitful statement often is delivered in a flat voice devoid of any real nuances.

The Mumbler

The words themselves may not be clear; they seem forced. This person is inclined to mumble and speak more softly than if he were passionate about his statement. Out of fear, however, it's possible that his voice may become higher and his rate of speech accelerated. Grammar and syntax may be off as well, with poor sentence structure and misspoken words likely to occur.

When Sarah professed her love for her fiancé, she would tell him how much she cared for him. And he would reply in a barely audible voice, simply repeating her words back to her. This didn't seem like a big deal until she started putting a few other things together. Instinctively we know that when a person responds like Sarah's ex, something is missing. And that something is often the truth.

Questions and Statements Shouldn't Sound Alike

Asking a question and making a statement have two distinct speaking styles. When a person asks a question—"What are you doing?"—his head comes up at the end—on the *ing* in *doing*. The eyes, too, will open wider at the last part of a question.

How is this useful? Suppose you get an answer that is

worded like a statement but styled like a question. This indicates that the person is unsure of his statement and is looking for confirmation from you. If you ask someone a question and he says with all certainty, "XYZ," but his voice, head, and eyes lift at the end of their statement, then his conviction is not as strong as he is leading you to believe.

SUMMARY

- Deceitful responses to questions regarding beliefs and attitudes take longer to think up.
- Watch out for reactions that are all out of proportion to the question.
- The person who is lying may leave out pronouns and speak in a monotonous and inexpressive voice. Words may be garbled, and syntax and grammar may be off. In other words, his sentences will likely be muddled.
- Statements sound an awful lot like questions, indicating that he's seeking reassurance.

SECTION 6

PSYCHOLOGICAL PROFILE

These clues concern how a liar thinks and what elements are usually missing from a story that's fictitious.

He's Got Cheating on His Mind

How people see the world is often a reflection of how they see themselves. If they think that the world is just a cesspool of lies and deceit, then they themselves may be full of lies and deceit. Watch out for those people who are always telling you just how corrupt the rest of the world is. As the saying goes, "It takes one to know one."

More specifically, if someone out of the blue with no real evidence accuses you of lying, ask yourself, "Why is he so paranoid?" In psychological terms this is what is referred to as projection. That's why the con artist is the first one to accuse another of cheating. If you're constantly being questioned about your motives or activities, this should send off bells in your mind. How often do we hear of a jealous boyfriend who constantly accuses his girlfriend of cheating on him only to have her find out later that he's guilty of everything he's been accusing her of doing?

Also, if he is always asking you if you believe him, then beware. Just as the clinically paranoid person feels that everyone can see right through him, this person questions the integrity of his facade. If your response gives no real indication of your thoughts, someone who is deceitful may respond with something like "You don't believe me, do you?"

Here's a good rule of thumb: most people who tell the truth expect to be believed.

CLUE 27

The Single Guy

Is the focus of the individual whose veracity you're trying to assess internal or external? Let's say a single man walks into a bar hoping to meet a woman. If he considers himself to be attractive and a good catch, then his focus would be on what the women in the bar look like. If he considers himself to be unattractive, then he would be more concerned with how he appears to them. In other words, his focus shifts depending upon his level of confidence.

When a person has confidence in his words, he's more interested in your understanding him and less interested in how he appears to you. This is a subtle clue, but we can see examples of this in everyday life. When you're interested simply in making a point, you want to make sure the other person understands you. When you're deceitful or trying to cover up, your focus is internal—on how you sound and appear as you're relating the "facts." You're conscious of your every word and movement. You try to act in a certain way so you will be perceived as you want to be. Subtle difference, but a big distinction.

CLUE 28

Another Dimension in Lying

Here's a clear indication of a story that doesn't ring true. As careful as he may be in relating the details of an event, the liar often leaves out one crucial element—the point of view or the opinion of someone else. This is because it adds another dimension or layer to his thinking that the liar is usually not clever enough to come up with. While other people may be included in his story, another person's *thoughts* are not. Suppose you ask your girlfriend where she was last night. She tells you she had to work late. But you're not convinced that's true. So you press for more information and ask what she had for dinner. Here are two possible answers she might give:

1. "Oh, I wasn't really hungry, so I just came home and watched TV with my roommate. She made pasta but I passed on it."
2. "Oh, I wasn't really hungry, so I just came home and watched TV. My roommate was so shocked that I would actually skip a meal, especially her famous pasta dish."

Both answers contain pretty much the same information, but the second adds another layer of thought—the roommate's point of view. Our gut instinct might tell us that this answer is more believable and more likely to be true than the first one. *Not* including another's point of view in an answer doesn't immediately disqualify it. The inclusion of another's point of view, though, will often indicate that you're being told the truth.

CLUE 29

Everything Went Perfectly!

One thing is almost always missing from a story that's not true—what went wrong. Events that are made up rarely include any negative details. A person who is lying is concerned with getting her story straight, and her thoughts are essentially one-dimensional. This means only primary thoughts—which are positive. Negation is not a primary emotion. In much the same way that if I said "Don't think of an elephant," you couldn't do it. In order to process the information, you need to first think of an elephant. Ask a friend to tell you about her last vacation. She'll cover all of the bases, both positive and negative—maybe the food was good, maybe the flight was delayed. Then ask someone to make up a story about a vacation that she never went on. You'll notice that the elements are usually all positive. The luggage never gets lost on a made-up voyage.

One caveat to this clue: if the story is used as an explanation as to why he was delayed or had to cancel plans, then obviously you can expect negatives. In that case this clue would not be helpful.

CLUE 30

Is There Anything *You* Would Like to Know?

A good liar may be practiced at answering questions so that she sounds truthful. But even the best will give herself away by not asking the right questions. The reason for this is that the conversation is not real for the liar. After all, she's not interested in learning anything. She only wants to convince you that she is being truthful. For example, during their first intimate encounter, Randy asks his new girlfriend if she's ever been tested for AIDS. She responds with "Oh, yes, certainly," and continues on a bit about annual checkups, giving blood, etc. And then nothing! If she was concerned about her health, as her answer implied, then she would have asked him the same question. The liar is often unaware that coming across as truthful means both answering and asking questions.

SUMMARY

- We often see the world as a reflection of ourselves. If you're being accused of something, check your accuser's veracity.
- Look at whether his focus is internal or external. When a person is confident about what he's saying, he's more interested in your understanding him and less interested in how he appears to you.
- The point of view of a third party is likely to be absent from a liar's story.
- In relating a story, a liar often leaves out the negative aspects.
- A liar willingly answers your questions but asks none of his own.

SECTION 7

GENERAL INDICATIONS OF DECEIT

The following is a mixed bag of clues that indicate deception. They can be used with great reliability by themselves or in conjunction with other clues.

CLUE 31

Whew, I'm Sure Glad That's Over

Watch and listen carefully during a conversation when the subject is changed. Does he become happier? Does he seem more relaxed? He may even offer a smile or nervous laugh.

Notice his posture. Does it become more relaxed and less defensive? The giveaway here is how fast and dramatically his mood changes, indicating his discomfort with the previous subject matter. Test him to see if he's quick to change the subject. If he has been accused of something abominable and is innocent, he will resent the accusations and will insist that the topic be explored further, either now or at some future date. Remember, the guilty wants the subject changed; the innocent always wants a further exchange of information.

How Dare You Accuse Me?

If he is accused of something harsh and is not indignant and offended that his honor has been questioned, this is a highly reliable sign that he's been caught off guard. It's been said that during the preliminary stages of the O. J. Simpson investigation, detectives thought it curious that Simpson did not appear to be outraged by the accusation that he had murdered his ex-wife and her friend Ron Goldman.

While he is being accused the liar will remain fairly expressionless, like a student being admonished by his principal. A look as if to say "What?!" will not be present. The liar is more concerned with how he is going to respond than he is with the accusation itself.

Never Believe Anyone Who Says This

Have you ever met someone who insisted on starting statements with phrases such as "To be perfectly honest," "To be frank," or "To tell you the truth"? Someone who is telling the truth doesn't need to convince you before he gets his words out. Some people habitually use these phrases. Such expressions mean literally that everything that came before them is a lie, everything that will come after will be a lie, but for now he's decided to pause to tell you the truth. If these phrases are not part of a person's usual verbal repertoire, watch out! If someone's going to tell you the truth, it's unlikely that he would start off by saying just that. If he feels the need to tell you that he's being honest and that you're about to receive the whole truth, you can be pretty sure you're not getting it.

Also included in this clue is the ever-pervasive and always annoying phrase "Why would I lie to you?" If you receive this response to an accusation you've made, be suspicious. If he's being accused of something, he probably has an excellent reason to lie.

I cannot tell a lie. Or can I? The phrase "I never lie" should always be received with caution. Anyone who needs to declare his virtuous nature does so because there is no other way for you to find out. Some people will say just about anything to sound believable, even lie straight to your face. One's honor should speak for itself. When a person tells you that he is the most honest person that you will ever meet, don't walk away—run.

CLUE 34

I've Got My Answer Down Pat

If his answer sounds pat and well rehearsed, there's a fair chance that he was expecting the question and took the time to get his story straight. Having facts and details at your fingertips that should not be easily recalled is a good indication that you have prepared. For instance, suppose Samantha, when asked where she was on a particular day two months ago, responds with, "I went to work, left at five-thirty, had dinner at Caracella's until seven forty-five, and then went straight home."

Law enforcement officers are aware of and use this clue with great results. Suppose a police detective questions a suspect. If the suspect is able to recall what he did and where he was on a given date two years earlier, something is very wrong. Most of us can't remember what we had for break-fast yesterday morning!

Rehearsed answers also provide a person with a way of giving you information that you never asked for, informa-tion that they want known. Politicians are famous for an-swering questions that were never asked. They have an agenda that will come out regardless of the questions put to them. Sometimes they don't even bother to rework the question; they just take off in their own direction. During the William Kennedy Smith rape trial, Smith's uncle Ted Kennedy was called as a defense witness to testify about to his knowledge of the day. In just minutes the courtroom was treated to Kennedy's taking us through the history of his family, the death of his brothers, and the trials and trib-ulations of his life. The courtroom was mesmerized. This was done to evoke the Kennedy aura and charm for the benefit of William Kennedy Smith. Whether it had a direct impact or not is hard to say, but Smith was found not guilty.

CLUE 35

Can You Repeat the Question, Please?

Instead of hemming and hawing, he may resort to one of the following statements to buy himself some time, to review the best course of action, to prepare his answer, or to shift the topic entirely. They are all designed to delay his answer. For example, you ask someone hold old he is and he responds with "How old do you think I am?" It's obvious that your answer may influence his. Here are some of the more popular ones.

1. "Could you repeat the question?"
2. "It depends on how you look at it."
3. "What's your point exactly?"
4. "Why would you ask something like that?"
5. "Where did you hear that?"
6. "Where is this coming from?"
7. "Could you be more specific?"
8. "How dare you ask me something like that?"
9. "I think we both know the answer to that."
10. "Well, it's not so simple as yes or no."
11. "That's an excellent question. It deserves some thought."
12. "Can you keep a secret? Great. So can I."
13. "I'm not sure this is the best place to discuss this."
14. The person repeats your question back to you, an attempt at sounding incredulous. For example, "Did I sell you a puppy with a heart condition? Is that what you're asking me?"

Sleight of Mouth

You've heard the old saying "If it sounds too good to be true, then it probably is." During the O. J. Simpson trial, Detective Mark Fuhrman said on the witness stand and under oath that he had never in the past ten years used a specific racial epithet. Almost no one—including the jury—believed that this was true. He would have been deemed as much more credible had he admitted to using racial epithets on occasion and with regret. But saying he never used them in any context seemed highly implausible. And indeed, the evidence later proved him to be a liar, forcing him to assert his Fifth Amendment privilege to avoid self-incrimination. If something sounds implausible, investigate further—no matter how convincing the person is.

Tricky Dicky

There is also such a thing as a lie through implication instead of expression. During the 1960 presidential campaign, Richard Nixon sought to remind Americans that his opponent John F. Kennedy was Catholic, not Protestant. We had never had a Catholic president before, and Nixon thought the fact that Kennedy was Catholic might make the American people uneasy. Blatantly reminding the public of his opponent's religion would make him look bad. So, in keeping with his reputation and according to the wisdom of politics, Nixon said the following: "I don't want anyone not to vote for John Kennedy because he is a Catholic." The intent was obviously different from the message, but he got his point across nicely. Although as history later proved, his effort was futile.

Whenever someone makes a point of telling you what they're *not* doing, you can be sure it's exactly what they *are* doing. The preamble is what they really mean. After a blind date, Jim was informed by the woman he went out with that she's very busy for the next few weeks but that she doesn't want him to think she's blowing him off. If that was not her intention, then it wouldn't have occurred to her to say that. When you hear, "Not to hurt your feelings, but . . ." you can be sure that this person doesn't mind hurting your feelings.

Another clever way of lying through implying comes in the form of a denial. It works like this. Let's say that an agent is attempting to convince a casting director to cast his client, John Jones, instead of another actor, Sam Smith. The agent casually mentions to the casting director that Sam was at the Betty Ford Clinic last month, but heard it was only to see a friend. Now the casting director wonders if Sam has an alcohol or drug problem. Had the agent simply said that Sam was there to get treatment, the casting director would have been suspicious of his intentions in mentioning it. By stating it in the form of a denial, he implants the suggestion without suspicion.

Let's look at another example. You hear, "He's having marital problems, but it has nothing to do with his wife's new job." What's the first thing you ask? "What does his wife do?" Suddenly you're in the exact conversation that is "supposed" to have no bearing on the facts. Clever, isn't it? Don't be misled.

CLUE 38

Don't Be Ridiculous

Beware of the person who uses humor and sarcasm to defuse your concerns. For instance, you ask one of your salespeople if she met with the competition and she replies, "Sure did. We meet every day in a secret warehouse. You can get in only if you know the special knock. It's there where we discuss the eventual downfall of your business empire." This makes you feel foolish about inquiring further. And she knows it. When you ask a serious question, you should expect a direct response.

CLUE 39

We're Out of Stock

Have you ever had the salesman tell you that the item you were looking for is inferior to another one? And as it turns out, the one that you want happens to be out of stock.

Clearly, he would have been much more believable if he had said he did have what you wanted but preferred to show you something even better. So before you accept someone at his word that he has something better to offer, first see whether he has what you originally asked for. If he doesn't, there's a better than even chance that you shouldn't believe him.

CLUE 40

The Number Zone

There's an old saying that goes, "If you always tell the truth, then you'll never have to remember anything." When a liar speaks, in an attempt to appear fluid, he will often fall into the number zone. This is when all of the numbers he mentions are the same or multiples of one another. This happens because he is thinking fast and is trying to remember what he's saying. A typical exchange during a job interview might go as follows:

Ms. SMITH: So, Mark, how many years' experience do you have in restaurant management?

MARK: At the three places I've worked, I've had about six years experience in total.

Ms. SMITH: Tell me a little bit about your experience at these places.

MARK: Well, I would put in sixty-hour weeks. And I was in charge of a crew of about twelve . . .

Watch out when facts, figures, and information have unusual similarities.

Nervous Nellie

While we can control some gestures, the following are involuntary responses that we have little or no control over:

The fight-or-flight syndrome: A person's face may become flushed or, with extreme fear, can turn white. Look for signs of rapid breathing and increased perspiration. Additionally, take note if he is trying to control his breathing to calm himself. This will appear as deep, audible inhaling and exhaling.

Trembling or shaking in voice and body: His hands may tremble. If he is hiding his hands, it might be an attempt to hide uncontrollable shaking. His voice may crack and seem inconsistent.

This is hard to swallow: Swallowing becomes difficult, so look for a hard swallow. Television or movie actors who wish to express fear or sadness often use this behavior—hence the expression "all choked up." Also indicative is a clearing of the throat. Due to anxiety, mucus forms in the throat. A public speaker who is nervous often clears his throat before speaking.

A choir boy, he's not! Vocal chords, like all muscles, tighten when a person is stressed. This will produce a higher sound, octave, and/or pitch.

I'm sorry, you said what? When we're under stress, our ability to focus on something is often diminished. Have you ever met someone at a party and forgotten his name right after you're introduced? Look for signs of distraction and an inability to pay attention to what's going on.

The whistler: Whistling seems to be a universal action to relax oneself when one is frightened or anxious, and is an unconscious attempt to build up courage or confidence. Most people have little *tells*—gestures used when they are nervous. They may rub an ear for reassurance or plaster on a fake smile to boost their confidence.

CLUE 42

Oh So Clever

The ancient sport of Judo has a fundamental philosophy: do not confront force with force; instead use your opponent's strength and turn it against him. The purveyors of this clue never get defensive or argue, they simply use your own words to support their claim.

Let's say that a guard is standing watch over a restricted area. It's his job to check ID's of those who enter. "I'm not sure you have authorization," he says to a man attempting access. "I'm not surprised," answered the man, "only a few people are aware of my clearance level. My work here is not supposed to be known by everyone."

Do you see how quickly the man verbally disarmed the guard? Had he started to argue and insist that he had clearance and that the guard was a fool for not knowing, he would have met with a wall of resistance. Rather, he agrees with the guard, and explains that the reason why the guard thought he didn't have authorization is the very reason why he *does* have authorization.

A certain bagel company overcame an obvious marketing problem by using this same practice. The company sells frozen bagels, yet it wanted to project an image of freshness, a characteristic that to most of us is the opposite of frozen. Their solution? The slogan "They taste best because they're frozen." Watch out when someone tries to use an obvious fact to support a questionable assertion.

CLUE 43

The Moral Assumption

This clue is so clever and pervasive that once you hear about it, you'll probably realize that it has already been used on you many times. The genesis of this clue comes courtesy of human nature. We all have an inherent need for order, for continuity and consistency.

The purveyor of deceit demonstrates characteristics with a specific moral bent so that other of his actions will be seen in that light. An example will clarify. Let's say that Joe, the financial officer of a large corporation, thinks that you may be on to his embezzlement scheme. He knows that you have no real proof, but he wants to throw you off the track. What might he do? In your presence, he may openly chastise another employee for "borrowing" some office supplies for her personal use at home. Your impression is that Joe is a moral person who objects to something as minor as stealing office supplies. Certainly he cannot be responsible for a large-scale embezzlement scheme.

A wife who is concerned that her husband suspects her of having a brief affair (which she did indeed have) might say something like this: "Honey, do you remember Harvey, Sally's husband? Well, Jill told me that they're having problems because Harvey kissed a coworker at the Christmas party. If you ask me, she should leave that no-good piece of garbage. Who knows what else he's done? Even if that was it, what is going through his mind? What an idiot!"

This is going to put serious doubts in the mind of this woman's husband that she would ever be unfaithful to him.

Oh, by the Way

Beware if she casually tells you something that should deserve more attention. For example, she says, "Oh, by the way, I've got to go out of town next weekend on busi-ness." If she doesn't usually travel for work on the week-ends, then you would expect her to make a point of how unusual the trip is. Her downplaying the trip makes it suspicious.

When something out of the ordinary happens and the person doesn't draw attention to, it means that she is try-ing to draw attention away from it. And for this there is usually a reason. Another tactic is running off a long list of items in the hope that one will remain unnoticed. Magicians, who are experts at slight-of-hand, know that their effectiveness lies in their ability to draw your at-tention where they want it to go. When your attention is being directed one way, check to see what lies the other way.

CLUE 45

Lots of Lies

If you catch a person in one lie, it makes good sense to question everything else that person has said. Let's say you're buying a car and the salesman says that you must act quickly because two other people have looked at this car and it's the last one in stock. Say something like "I hear that this model retains its value better than most others, isn't that true?" Or "I heard that they're going to raise the prices on next year's model substantially." These are statements an honest salesperson will question if he or she hasn't heard any such thing. However, if your salesperson is quick to agree with you, it means that he would say almost anything to make the sale—which also means that he probably doesn't have anyone else interested in the car, even though he's claimed otherwise. If you can, try to find out if this person has a reputation for being deceitful. Honesty is a function of character, and character is not something that is easily changed.

Wild, Wild, Wild

"You're not going to believe what happened to me!" How many times have we heard that phrase? Common sense dictates that if we want someone to believe us, we should make our story or explanation as believable as possible. This is usually true, but not always. Sometimes the more outrageous a story is, the more believable it becomes. Why? Because we think to ourselves, *If this person wanted to lie to me, he'd probably have come up with something a little less far-fetched.* So in this clever deception the liar embellishes his story and simply offers the phrase "Don't you think that if I was going to lie to you, I'd come up something a little more believable? You just can't make this stuff up." When in fact that's exactly what he's done.

SUMMARY

- When the subject is changed, he's in a better, more relaxed mood.
- He does not become indignant when falsely accused.
- He uses such phrases as "To tell you the truth," "To be perfectly honest," and "Why would I lie to you?"
- He has an answer to your question down pat.
- He stalls by asking you to repeat the question or by answering your question with a question.
- What he's saying sounds implausible.
- He offers a preamble to his statement starting with "I don't want you to think that . . ." Often that's exactly what he wants you to think.
- She uses humor or sarcasm to defuse your concerns.
- He offers you a "better" alternative to your request when he is unable to give you what you originally asked for.
- All of his facts relating to numbers are the same or multiples of one another.
- There is evidence of involuntary responses that are anxiety based.
- He uses an obvious fact to support a dubious action.
- She casually tells you something that deserves more attention.
- He exclaims his displeasure at the actions of another who has done something similar so that you will not suspect him.

- If he lies about one thing, everything he says is questionable.
- His story is so wild that you almost don't believe it. But you do, because if he wanted to lie, you think that he would have come up with something more plausible.

BECOMING A HUMAN LIE DETECTOR

"Deceit, feeding on ignorance, weaves carelessly around
the truth, twisting its prey down a path
to destined regret."
—DAVID J. LIEBERMAN

This part contains a sophisticated and comprehensive system of questioning that will get the truth out of any person. We often go into verbal combat unprepared to do battle. Because we're unable to think clearly and effectively communicate our thoughts, we think of what we should have said two days later.

The clues to deception can be used with great reliability in everyday situations and conversations. However, if you must know the truth in a given situation, this part provides you with a sequence of questions that virtually guarantees that you will know (a) if you're being lied to and (b) what the truth is if it's not obvious from the lie. This procedure was developed as a result of my research in human behavior. When used in order, all three phases offer you the greatest opportunity to get at the truth.

OUTLINE

Phase One. *Three Attack-Sequence Primers*

Sometimes this technique in and of itself will reveal a person's guilt, but if it doesn't, you haven't lost any leverage and can proceed to phase two. The primers are used to test a person's vulnerability and to gauge his or her level of concern over a particular subject.

Phase Two. *Eleven Attack Sequences*

This phase consists of one direct sequence and ten other possible sequences. Use whichever one best fits the situation. These carefully scripted sequences put you in the best possible position to get at the truth. You will see that the phrasing of your request—what precedes the request and what follows it—is essential. Context is everything!

Phase Three. *Eleven Silver Bullets*

Fire these off if you're still not satisfied. Perhaps the person hasn't yet confessed but you know he isn't being truthful. If you feel you've been lied to, but a full confession isn't forthcoming, this phase takes you through an additional process to get to the truth. Though these bullets can be fired in any order you want, some will rule out others. So choose ahead of time which are most appropriate for the situation.

HOW TO PROCEED

Lay the groundwork by starting with phase one. Then choose one of the eleven attack sequences from phase two. If you haven't gotten a full confession after you try an attack sequence, fire your silver bullets one by one. The results will be truly astonishing.

If terms like *arsenal*, *weapons*, and *bullets* seem warlike, it's understandable. But they're thoroughly appropriate considering the situation. A lie can be very injurious. Protecting yourself is the objective. You need to see the process of detecting deceit for what it really is—a verbal battle. And from now on, when you enter this battle, you will be very well armed.

PHASE 1

THREE ATTACK-SEQUENCE PRIMERS

Most of us are familiar with the Rorschach test, developed in 1921 by Hermann Rorschach. The test consists of ten bilaterally symmetrical inkblots, each on an individual card. These abstract shapes, which have no particular meaning or form, are shown one at a time to the subject. Put simply, the theory behind the test is that a person's interpretation of the shapes will reveal his or her unconscious or sublimated thoughts.

For the sequence primers, we use the same psychological principles but employ them in a whole new way: you find out what's on a person's mind by giving him a *verbal* abstract test. A person's true intentions will surface in his comments and/or gestures.

PRIMER 1

Don't Accuse—Allude

Asking a person outright, "Have you been cheating on me?" will put him on the defensive. The objective here is to ask a question that does not *accuse* the person of anything but *alludes* to the person's possible behavior.

If he doesn't realize you're implying anything, then he's probably not guilty. But if he gets defensive, then he *knows* what you're getting at. The only way he could know is if he is guilty of the accusation. The point is, an innocent person shouldn't have a clue about what you're alluding to.

You don't want the question to be accusatory or too broad. For example, if you suspect someone of murder, you wouldn't say, "Kill anyone last weekend?" And asking, "How was your day?" is clearly too broad.

You want the question to be framed in such a way that he will get suspicious of your asking only if he is guilty. He won't react unusually if he isn't, but as if it were an out-of-the-ordinary question. If you asked your neighbor whether space aliens had landed on her front lawn, you wouldn't expect her to respond seriously at all. She may answer jokingly or just laugh it off entirely. And you certainly wouldn't expect, "Why do you ask? Did someone say something to you?" This response is curious for a question that should be taken as absurd.

When you ask the question, be matter-of-fact. Don't square off. You don't want him defensive unless he has a reason to be. Beware of all the clues to deceit, particularly the one about a guilty person continuing to add more information as he thinks of it and without your prompting.

Now, whatever is on the person's mind will reveal itself in the conversation that ensues. If he's innocent of what you suspect him of, then he'll answer casually and leave it at that. However, if he's guilty he will want to know what you're thinking because he's not sure why you're asking the question. So he'll question you about your question.

Examples of Phrasing Perimeters

The key is to phrase a question that sounds perfectly innocent to an innocent person, but like an accusation to the guilty.

SUSPICION: You think that your employee was fired from his last job because he stole from his previous employer.

QUESTION: "Do you still keep in contact with your old boss?"

SUSPICION: You feel that your boyfriend or girlfriend was unfaithful the night before.

QUESTION: "Anything interesting happen last night?"

SUSPICION: You think a coworker told your secretary that you have a crush on her.

QUESTION: "Heard any good gossip recently?"

Any answers such as "Why do you ask?" or "Where did you hear that?" indicate concern on the person's part. He should not be seeking information from you if he does not think that your question is leading. He should also not be interested in why you're asking the question unless he thinks that you may know what he doesn't want you to.

Similar Scenario

This primer works by introducing a scenario similar to what you suspect is going on. There are two ways to do this— specific and general. This primer deals with specifics, while Primer 3 takes the general approach. This works well because you're able to bring up the topic without being accusatory.

SUSPICION: You suspect one of your salespeople has lied to a customer in order to make the sale.

QUESTION: "Jim, I'm wondering if you could help me with something. It's come to my attention that someone in the sales department has been misrepresenting our products to customers. How do you think we can clear this up?"

If he's innocent of the charges he's likely to offer his advice and be pleased that you sought out his opinion. If he's guilty he'll seem uncomfortable and will assure you that he *never* do anything like that. Either way, this opens the door to probe further.

SUSPICION: A hospital administrator suspects that a doctor was drinking while on duty.

QUESTION: "Dr. Marcus, I'd like to get your advice on something. A colleague of mine at another hospital has a problem with one of her doctors. She feels he may be drinking
while on call. Do you have any suggestions on how she
can approach the doctor about this problem?"

Again, if he's guilty he'll seem very uncomfortable. If he's
not drinking on duty, then he will be pleased that you sought
his advice and offer it.

PRIMER 3

It's Amazing, Isn't It?

With this primer, you still bring up the subject, but in a
general way. Casually broaching the subject in this manner
provides great insight into the person's innocence or guilt.

SUSPICION: You think a student has cheated on her exam.
QUESTION: "Isn't it amazing how someone can cheat on a
test and not realize that I was standing behind her the
entire time?"
SUSPICION: You suspect a coworker of bad-mouthing you to
your boss.
QUESTION: "It's amazing all the backstabbing that goes on
around here, isn't it? And these people doing it think that
it won't get back to the person involved."

SUSPICION: You think that your girlfriend may be two-timing you.

QUESTION: "It's amazing how someone can be unfaithful and expect not to get caught."

Again, any answers that prompt a response such as "Why do you ask?" Or "Where did you hear that?" show that your question concerns him.

Sometimes there's no need to confront someone who we feel has lied. We just want to know for ourselves. In instances like these, it's not necessary to finish the attack sequence. Just use the primers to satisfy your own curiosity, or use the techniques in Part 3, which allow you to discreetly gather information.

Note: Two other responses are possible for primers 2 and 3. The person may begin to talk generically about the subject or change it completely. A change in subject is highly indicative of guilt. However, if he finds your question interesting and he's innocent, he might begin a conversation about it. This is a strong indication of his innocence, because he's unafraid to discuss the subject and hasn't probed why you have even brought it up.

PHASE 2

ELEVEN ATTACK SEQUENCES

It's 8:00 A.M. on a Sunday morning. You're resting in bed when the doorbell rings. Mumbling incoherently, you get up, put on your robe, and stagger to the door. Upon opening it you're greeted by a smiling, energetic young women waving a glossy pamphlet in your face and asking for thirty seconds of your time. Ten minutes later you close the door, stumble back to bed, and ask yourself, "Why did I give that woman ten dollars to save the red-spotted frog from extinction? I don't even like frogs." Obviously there was something involved that made you exchange something you like—your money—for something you don't particularly care about—frogs. You can see from this transaction that sometimes it's the context of a request, not the request itself, that determines a person's willingness to cooperate or resist.

ATTACK SEQUENCE 1

Direct Questioning

Sometimes the direct approach is best. The only drawback to asking a question outright is that you then can't use any of the other sequences unless you let a considerable amount of time pass.

Stage 1. Ask your question directly. When you talk with the person you want to get information from, to maximize the amount you learn, follow these six guidelines.

1. Give no advance warning of the subject you're about to bring up or of any feelings of mistrust you may have. Unsolicited questions are the toughest for him to answer, so if he brings up the subject, make sure that you ask your question *after* any statements that he may make. His deceit will be harder to detect if:

- He has responded to the same statement before. When you ask your question, phrase it in a new way. Don't keep asking the same question over and over again. He gets entrenched in his position and good at convincing you. By varying how you ask your question, you have more opportunities to detect deceit.

- He knows that he will be asked the question. Give no warning of what's on your mind.

- He knows what he's going to say, like an actor reading his lines. You know they are not his words; he's just following a script. Give him some time and you'll be crying and laughing along with him. No matter how trained he is, once he gets beyond the script, he's unrehearsed and unprepared, and that's right where you want him.

- He thinks he's justified in lying. This removes all guilt-oriented clues. When people believe *in* what they are saying—even if they don't believe *it*—they say it with conviction.

- He feels there's little or nothing at stake, so he probably won't appear nervous, which means you can't use those clues as an indicator. Most of the other clues will still be available for you to observe.

- He has a severe mental disorder. Such a person does not have a concept of right and wrong.

2. Never reveal what you know first. Ask questions to gather information to see if it's consistent with what you already know. During World War II, England had cracked Enigma, the secret code used by the Germans. England learned of an impending attack by the Germans on the town of Coventry. However, if Churchill evacuated the people, the Germans would know that England had broken the code and would change it. This left Churchill with an obvious conundrum. Weighing the lives of those who lived in Coventry against the enormous possible future gain of being privy to all Germany's war plans, Churchill decided not to tell the townspeople, and hundreds died. With any luck you'll never be in such a predicament, but you can see that sometimes it's better not to reveal your position—even if it means suffering great short-term losses.

The greater objective must be kept in mind. This makes it possible for him to slip up and reveal information you know to be contradictory to the truth. If he knows what you know, then he can tailor his story to be consistent with the information that you already know.

3. The way you present yourself can greatly influence the attitude of the other person. Simple things such as unbuttoning your coat or uncrossing your arms can make the

other person feel less defensive. When you have a rapport with someone, he is much more likely to feel comfortable and open up. Rapport creates trust, allowing you to build a psychological bridge to the person. The conversation is likely to be more positive and you will be much more persuasive. Three powerful tips for establishing and building rapport are:

- *Matching posture and movements:* If he has one hand in his pocket, you put your hand in yours. If he makes a gesture with his hand, after a moment, you casually make the same gesture.
- *Matching speech:* Try to match his rate of speech. If he's speaking in a slow, relaxed tone, you do the same. If he's speaking quickly, then you speak quickly.
- *Matching key words:* If she is prone to using certain words or phrases, employ them when you speak. For instance, if she says, "The offer is designed for incredible gain for both parties," later in the conversation you might say something like, "I like that the offer is designed to offer incredible gain . . ." Make sure that you don't seem to be mimicking her. Obvious copying of another's movements is unproductive. A simple reflection of aspects of the person's behavior or speech is enough. This can be a very powerful skill for you, once you become good at it.

Later in the questioning you'll move to stage four. This will make your target person nervous, enabling you to shift strategies. But initially you don't want to make him nervous.

You want to create an environment in which the only reason he has to be nervous is if he's done something wrong. This way any anxiety-based responses or actions are the product of his deceit, not his environment.

4. Lie detectors use what is called a baseline, which corresponds to the person's normal level of anxiety. It's a good idea, if possible, to do something similar. Ask a question that you know will produce a response similar to how you expect him to react. You need to know whether certain patterns of behavior are part of this person's usual repertoire. You want to establish how he responds to a question that can be answered easily and use that as a benchmark if you don't know the person well. In other words, if he waves his arms around no matter what he's talking about, you want to know this.

5. Although your posture should be relaxed and non-threatening, see if you can square off so that you're facing each other. This allows you to use several of the detection clues having to do with body language (see part 1, section 1 and 2).

6. Never, ever interrupt. You can't learn anything new while you're talking. Also ask open-ended questions. This gives you the opportunity to hear longer answers.

If you don't get the answer you're looking for, continue to the next stage.

Stage 2. Silence. First, don't respond at all. This will usually make him continue talking. The guilty abhor silence. It makes them uncomfortable. It also gives you a chance to observe other clues such as changes of subject, uncomfortable laughter, nervousness, etc.

If you don't get the answer you're looking for, continue to the next stage.

Stage 3. Really? At the end of his answer respond with "Really?" This one simple word gives you two shots at assessing the same answer. He doesn't know how you feel about his answer yet, so it doesn't tip your hand. But it forces him to repeat his response. Here, you'll look for clues such as if his voice goes up at the end of the sentence (see clue 25), indicating he may be unconsciously looking for confirmation.

If you don't get the answer you're looking for, continue to the next stage.

Stage 4. Sudden death. Follow with "Is there anything you want to get off your chest?" This puts him on the defensive. Now you can watch for those clues that come out when the person is more nervous than before you challenged his credibility. This question really confuses people because the answer is going to be no, regardless. But now that you've changed the tone of the conversation, he's thrown for a loop.

If you don't get the answer you're looking for, continue to phase three.

Lead and Confine

Stage 1. Ask a leading question. Ask a question that restricts his answer to something he feels is positive, a question he doesn't mind answering truthfully. This technique is called lead and confine. For example, if you want to know if your boyfriend went out last night, an outright question might make him lie if he feels you will be upset. Instead, your question is "You were back by two A.M. last night, weren't you?" If he didn't go out, he would be free to tell you. But if he did, he feels comfortable agreeing with you because you make it sound okay. Whether he was or wasn't back by two A.M. isn't the point. You've got the answer to your real question.

Let's take another example. If you want know if your fiancée ever cheated on you, the question you would ask is "You were only with other people *before* we got engaged, right?" Again, she feels that she's comforting you by answering the way you've indicated is okay. Even though she answers yes, she still could have cheated on you *after* you got engaged as well. So if you want to know that, too, make that the focus of your next attack. After some time has passed, you might ask, "I know that you've had to get some things out of your system, but when we get married, I want to know that I can trust you. You will give up these ways once we're married, won't you?"

If you don't get the answer you're looking for, continue to the next stage.

Stage 2. Reverse course: You've got be kidding! Now you throw her completely off balance, putting her in a situation where she won't know how she should answer. Here you sound disappointed that she answered that way. This forces her to rethink her answer and become comfortable telling you the truth. You would say something like "I was hoping you did, so you would have gotten it out of your system. Please tell me that you've done it, so I know that it's over with."

If you don't get the answer you're looking for, continue to the next stage.

Stage 3. This is not going to work. This is where you let her know that everything you've ever thought about her may be wrong. The only way she can show you that she is the person you thought she was is to confess. "I thought you were somebody who had a sense of adventure. Someone who knows how to live a little."

If you don't get the answer you're looking for, continue to phase three.

ATTACK SEQUENCE 3

Time Line Distortion

This sequence combines several psychological principles and produces truly remarkable results. To explain, we'll use the following example. Let's say that your wife calls you up at work and informs you that your fifteen-year-old son took the family car for a joy ride and was just brought back by the police. You might be understandably upset. However, let's take the same set of circumstances, except for one thing. In a different conversation, your wife casually mentions that this mischievous deed was done by your now twenty-five-year-old son *ten years earlier*. Your reaction is likely to be considerably more mild. Why? Because time has passed.

Let's look at the flip side of this example. If a couple's son borrowed their car without permission ten years earlier, he would probably feel that he could mention it with full impunity—it might even be amusing at this point—and he certainly doesn't have to worry about being punished. It's doubtful, though, that he would feel so comfortable telling his parents if he had taken the car the night before.

Time is a powerful psychological tool that can shift our perspective dramatically. The two factors affecting time are when the event occurred and when you became aware of it. If either or both of these factors are moved into the past, the event is no longer timely. This greatly reduces its perceived significance.

Scenario A

In this example, you suspect your spouse of having an affair.

Stage 1. Setting the scene. Let the conversation turn casually to the topic of cheating. Then very nonchalantly joke about the affair that you suspect him of having had. This will prompt him to ask what you're talking about.

Stage 2. It's no big deal. Looking fairly shocked that he seems concerned, you reply with "Oh, I've always known about that. Do you want to know how I found out?" This question completely shifts the weight of the conversation. He feels that he's totally in the clear and will now seek to satisfy his curiosity. He's thinking that the relationship has been fine for all this time, even though you "knew" of his affair for some time.

If you don't get the answer you're looking for, continue to the next stage.

Stage 3. I appreciate what you've done. If he still denies it, tell him, "I thought that you knew I knew but were protecting my feelings, knowing that I'd understand it was just an accident and that I really wouldn't want to talk about it." Now it's even more tempting to confess because by doing so, he actually thinks that he's a good guy. And that all this time he was doing something nice and didn't even know it.

Scenario B

Let's take an example in which you suspect several employees in your store of stealing money.

Stage 1. Setting the scene. With one of the employees let the conversation turn casually to stealing and say, "Oh, I knew right from the start what was going on."

Stage 2. It's no big deal. "You had to know I knew. How else do you think you could have gotten away with it

for so long? I hope you don't think I'm a complete idiot."
(That's a great phrase because he doesn't want to risk of-
fending you on top of everything else.)

Stage 3. I appreciate what you've done. "I know that
you were just going along with it because you were scared
of what the others would do. It's really okay. I know you're
not that kind of person." Do you see how nicely this works?
By confessing he feels that he's being a good person, the
kind of person his boss thinks he is.

*If you don't get the answer you're looking for, continue
to phase three.*

Direct Assumption/Shot in the Dark

Stage 1. Set the scene. This sequence is used when you
have a gut feeling that something isn't right, but you're not
quite sure what it is and you don't have any evidence to
support your thinking. In this sequence he is forced to talk
about whatever he feels are his misdeeds. You will be
amazed at what comes out of his mouth. Remember to hold
your ground and not settle until you hear a confession of
value. We've all done things we're not proud of. This questioning sequence really opens the mental floodgates. You
have the leverage because you're in control of the conversation—you're holding all the cards. It's his job to figure out

what he's done wrong and how to make it all right. First set the scene: be somewhat curt and standoffish, as if something heavy-duty is bothering you. This will cause his mind to race to find ways to explain the "error of his ways."

Stage 2. I'm hurt. Say, "I've just found something out and I'm really hurt [shocked/surprised]. I know you're going to lie to me and try to deny it, but I just wanted you to know that I know." This is different from saying, "Don't lie to me." By saying "I know you're going to lie," you establish that (a) he's guilty of something and (b) you know what it is. Now it's merely a question of whether or not he comes clean. Notice that you're not asking for anything. Saying "Please don't lie to me" establishes that you don't know what the truth is, putting you in a weaker position.

If you don't get the answer you're looking for, continue to the next stage.

Stage 3. Holding your ground. Say, "I think we both know what I'm talking about. We need to clear the air, and we can start by your talking."

If you don't get the answer you're looking for, continue to the next stage.

Stage 4. Continue to hold your ground. Repeat phrases such as "I'm sure it will come to you" and "The longer I wait, the madder I'm getting."

If you don't get the answer you're looking for, continue to the next stage.

Stage 5. Apply social pressure. Now is the time to add a little social pressure. This reestablishes that your assertion is a *fact*, not a suspicion. "We were all talking about it. Everybody knows." Now he begins to get curious about who knows and how they found out. As soon as he tries to find out this information, you'll know that he's guilty.

If you don't get the answer you're looking, for continue to phase three.

Who, Me?

Stage 1. Setting the scene. This sequence works well when you don't have any real proof that someone has wronged you but you believe that you are right in your assumption of guilt. For example, lets say Winston's house had been broken into. He was convinced that his ex-girlfriend, whom he had recently broken up with, was the culprit. But he wasn't sure. She had his key, and the only thing that was missing was some expensive jewelry that was well hidden. But the housekeeper or the electrician who had just finished some work could have done it or it might have been simply a random burglary. Just calling his ex-girlfriend and accusing her of this crime would have been futile. She would deny all knowledge of the event, and he would be left with no evidence and no confession. Instead, he proceeded as follows.

He phoned to let her know in a very nonaccusatory way that there had been a break-in and some items were missing. In an attempt to sound surprised, she asked what happened. The following is a short example of the type of conversation that would ensue.

WINSTON: The police are going to want to talk to everyone who had access to the house. Since you still have a key, they're going to want to speak with you. Just routine stuff, I'm sure. Of course you're not a suspect.

EX-GIRLFRIEND: But I don't know anything about it.

WINSTON: Oh, I know. Just policy, I guess. Anyway, one of my neighbors said that she got a partial license-plate number on a car that was by my house that day.

EX-GIRLFRIEND: (*After a long pause*) Well, I was driving around your neighborhood that day. I stopped by to see if you were home. But when you weren't, I just left.

So far she has effectively explained her presence there that day. But in doing so she has established either an uncanny coincidence or her guilt. Had she been innocent, she would have had no reason to pursue this line of conversation. He then introduces more evidence.

WINSTON: Oh, really? Well, they did a fingerprint test too. That should show something.

EX: What test?

WINSTON: Oh, they dusted for prints and . . .

At this point she said that the police might pick up her prints, since she had been there previously. Although by now he knew she was involved, it wasn't until about ten minutes later that she broke down and confessed—at first to just being in the house and then later to taking the jewelry.

Stage 2. Inform nonaccusatorily. Casually inform your suspect of the situation.

Stage 3. Introduce evidence to be rebutted. As you introduce the evidence, look to see if every one of your statements are met by explanations from him as to how the evidence could be misunderstood. For example, let's say that you suspect that your coworker had shredded some of your files in hopes of beating you out for a promotion. You would first set the stage by letting him know that you can't find some important files. And then you say something like, "Well, it's a good thing my new secretary noticed someone by the shredder the other day. She said she recognized his face but didn't know his name." At this point see if he offers up a reason as to why he would be mistaken for the "real culprit." He might tell you that he was there shredding some of his own documents. An innocent person would not feel the need to explain in order to avert the possibility that he might be wrongly accused.

If you don't get the answer you're looking for, continue to the next stage.

Stage 4. Continue. Continue with more facts that the person can try to explain away. But in actuality, as soon as he starts to talk about why the situation might "look that way," you know you have him.

If you don't get the answer you're looking for, continue to phase three.

Outrageous Accusations

In this sequence you accuse the person of everything and anything under the sun. By accusing him of doing every possible thing wrong, you will get a confession concerning what he has really done—which to him at this point is no big deal, considering all that you're accusing him of.

Stage 1. Accuse him of everything. In a very fed-up manner accuse him of doing every imaginable dishonest and disloyal act.

Stage 2. Introduce the suspicion. Now you introduce the one thing that you feel he really has done, and in an attempt to clear himself of the other charges, he will offer an explanation for his one slip-up. He will of course naturally profess total innocence of the other accusations.

Phrase it as such: "I mean, it's not like you just [whatever you suspect him of doing], that would be fine. But all these other things are unspeakable."

You might get a response like "No, I just stole that one

file because of the pressure to get the job done, but I would never sell trade secrets!" The only way to prove his innocence to all of your outrageous accusations is to explain why he did what you really suspect him of doing.

If you don't get the answer you're looking for, continue to phase three.

Stage 3. Step in closer. This increases anxiety in the guilty. The movement makes him feel he's being closed in on. If you don't get the answer you want, go back to stage 1 and ask again.

If you don't get the answer you're looking for, continue to phase three.

Is There a Reason?

Stage 1. Introduce a fact. In this sequence the person must answer your question with information, not a simple denial. For example, if you want to know if your secretary went out last night when she said she was sick, your question might be "I drove by your house on the way home. Is there a reason your car wasn't in the driveway?" If you simply ask, "Did you go out last night?" she can deny that she did. But by introducing a plausible fact, you force her to answer. If she was out, she will try to explain the missing car. When she does, you will have verified what you suspect to be true— that she was not at home sick. Do you see how this works? If she lied about having to stay home because she was sick, then she has to explain where the car was. She might say that a friend borrowed it or that she ran out to get cold medicine, etc. Had she been home sick, she would simply tell you that you were wrong—the car was in the driveway.

Stage 2. One more shot. You want to give her one more shot at coming clean or at coming up with a reasonable explanation to explain your "fact." Say, "Oh, that's odd, I called your house and I got your machine." To which she might reply, "Oh, I turned my machine on to get some rest." Remember, if she is guilty she will look for any way to make her story fit your facts. If she does this, she's probably lying. Now it's possible that a friend did borrow the car and that she did turn her machine off. However, at some point these "explanations" are going to start sounding manufactured.

Additionally, because she is forced to tell new lies to protect previous ones, you now have several statements you can look at for signs of deceit.

If you don't get the answer you're looking for, continue to the next stage.

Stage 3. Stare. Staring is an underused yet formidable weapon. It produces different results depending upon particular situations. Staring makes someone who is on the defensive feel closed in; your glare is infringing on her personal space, inducing a mental claustrophobia. To escape she needs only tell you the truth. Lock eyes with her and ask again.

If you don't get the answer you're looking for, continue to phase three.

Third-Party Confirmation

This sequence is one of the more powerful ones, provided you have the cooperation of a third party. You gain maximum credibility, because it removes just about any doubt that there is deception on your part.

Scenario

You suspect one of your employees is having someone else punch out on the time clock for him.

Stage 1. Accuse outright. After gaining the assistance of a friend or coworker, you have this person make the accusation for you. Such as "Mel, I was talking to Cindy, and she told me she's getting pretty tired of your having someone else punch out for you so you can leave work early."

At this point Mel is concerned only with Cindy's disapproval of his actions. Your friend is thoroughly believable because we rarely think to question this type of third-party setup.

If you don't get the answer you're looking for, continue to the next stage.

Stage 2. Are you kidding? If he still won't confess, switch the focus with "Are you kidding? It's common knowledge, but I think I know how you can smooth things over with her." See if he takes the bait. A person who's innocent would not be interested in smoothing things over with someone else for something that he hasn't done.

If you don't get the answer you're looking for, continue to the next stage.

Stage 3. Last call. "Okay. But are you sure?" At this point any hesitation is likely to be sign of guilt because he's quickly trying to weigh his options.

If you don't get the answer you're looking for, continue to phase three.

ATTACK SEQUENCE 9

The Chain Reaction

In this sequence you create a chain reaction that originates in the person's own deceitful actions. In other words, the only way he can take advantage of a new opportunity presented to him is to admit his previous actions. The sequence is based on the assumption that the wrongdoing took place and brings the conversation past that. Whenever you want a confession, you're far better off moving the conversation past his actions. Otherwise he's likely to lie or become defensive. Both reactions do you little good. However, if the focus of your discussion is not on what he has already done, then you're likely to get him to admit to his actions, as he assumes that you already have proof of them.

Scenario

You suspect several employees in your store of stealing money.

Stage 1. Setting the scene. In a one-on-one meeting with the employee, let them know that you're looking for someone to be in charge of a new internal theft program for the entire company.

Stage 2. The irony is . . . "We're looking for someone who knows how it's done. Now don't worry, you're not going to get in trouble. As a matter of fact we've known about it for some time. We were more interested in seeing how efficient you were. Quite impressive. Anyway, we feel that since you know how it's done, you'll know how to prevent it. Granted, it's pretty unusual, but this is an unusual instance."

He now feels comfortable with his previous actions. His new position is even dependent upon his misdeeds. Denying what he's done will cost him his big promotion. If you tell your story convincingly, he will even boast about his misdeeds.

If you don't get the answer you're looking for, continue to the next stage.

Stage 3. I told them so. "You know, I told them that you would be too afraid to have an open discussion about this. [Notice how disarming the phrase "open discussion" is; it's much better than "confess" or "stop lying."] They were wrong, I was right."

This works because he now feels that whoever "they" are, they're on his side. He's going to be hesitant about letting "them" down. Look for hesitation on his part. If he's guilty he will be weighing his options. This takes time. An innocent person has nothing to think about. Only the guilty have the option of confessing or not.

If you don't get the answer you're looking for, continue to phase three.

The Missing Link

This sequence is used when you have some idea about what's going on, but you don't have the full story. You offer the information you do have so that he believes the rest of what you say. This is also used with one magic key phrase, and if he take the bait, he's guilty.

Scenario

You think that your mother-in-law may have hired a private investigator to follow you around.

Stage 1. List facts. Tell her something that you know to be true. "I know you're not very fond of me, and that you objected to the wedding, but this time you've gone too far."

Stage 2. State your assumption. "I know all about the investigator. Why did you think that was necessary?"

Stage 3. The magic phrase. "You know what, I'm too upset to talk about this now."

If she becomes quiet she's probably guilty. If she has no idea what you're talking about, you can be sure that she doesn't care if you're too upset to talk about it—because you have no reason to be upset.

The guilty person will honor your request because she won't want to anger you further. An innocent person will be mad at you for accusing her of something that she hasn't done and will want to discuss it *now*.

If you don't get the answer you're looking for, continue to phase three.

Condemn or Concern

Stage 1. I'm just letting you know. The key with this sequence is not to accuse, just to inform. The response of your suspect will let you know if he's innocent or guilty.

This sequence explores a person's frame of mind when he or she is presented with new information. Pamela has a routine physical, and when her doctor gets the blood test results, he calls to inform her that she has contracted the herpes virus. Thinking back over her recent sexual partners, she is convinced that it must have been either Mike or Steven who gave her the disease. Merely asking her two "suspects" if they knowingly gave her herpes would probably prove futile, as a denial by both would be likely. Fortunately Pamela is skilled in the art of detecting deceit and decides on a different course of action.

She calls both guys up and casually informs them that she just found out that she has herpes. The responses she got led her straight to the culprit. After hearing the news the two men responded as follows:

MIKE: Well, don't look at me. I didn't give it to you! I'm clean.

STEVEN: You what! How long have you had it for? You might have given it to me! I can't believe this. Are you sure?

Which one is likely to be the guilty party? If you guessed Mike, you're right. On hearing that his previous sexual partner has an incurable, easily transmissible disease, he goes on the defensive—assuming that he is being accused of giving it to her. He is unconcerned about his own health because he already *knows* he is infected. Steven, in contrast, assumes that the call is to inform him that she might have infected *him*. Thus, he gets angry because he is concerned about his health. Mike simply wants to make Pamela believe he is not guilty.

Here's another example. Let's say that you're working in the customer service department of a computer store. A customer brings back a nonworking printer for an exchange, claiming that he bought it just few days before. He has the all-important receipt and the printer is packed neatly in the original box. Upon inspecting the contents you find that a necessary, expensive, and easily removable component of the machine is missing, a clear indication of why the machine was not functioning properly. Here are two possible responses you might get after informing the customer of your discovery.

Response 1. "I didn't take it out. That's how it was when I bought it." (Defensive)

Response 2. "What? You sold me a printer that has a missing part? I wasted two hours trying to get that thing to work." (Offensive)

Do you see how effective this is? The person who utters Response 2 has every right to be annoyed; it never crosses his mind that he's being accused of anything. The person who gives Response 1 knows he never even *tried* to get the printer to work because he took the part out. It doesn't occur to him to become angry. He assumes that he's being accused of removing the part and becomes defensive when you inform him the part is missing.

If you don't get the answer you're looking for, continue to phase three.

ELEVEN SILVER BULLETS: HOW TO GET THE TRUTH WITHOUT BEATING IT OUT OF THEM

The following eleven bullets can be used independently or in order, one after another, until you get the answer you're looking for. They are designed to get the person to confess. While the bullets can be fired in any order, some of them negate subsequent ones, so see which ones are appropriate for your particular situation and then arrange them in the appropriate sequence.

You want to convey enthusiasm and truthfulness when you use these bullets. They are most effective when you convey complete honesty in what you're saying. So don't "give yourself away" by making the same mistakes revealed in the clues. You see, the clues to deceit work in reverse as well. If you do not commit any of them, the person you are speaking to will at both the conscious and the unconscious level perceive you as truthful. Don't forget that this person must believe what you're saying is true. If you threaten to do something, it has to be a believable threat or he won't take the bait. To convey honesty and truthfulness in your message, use the following techniques:

- Look the person directly in the eyes.
- Use hand movements to emphasize your message.
- Use animated gestures that are fluid and consistent with the conversation.

- Stand or sit upright—no slouching.
- Don't start off with any statements such as "To tell you the truth . . ." or "To be perfectly honest with you . . ."
- Face the person straight on. Don't back away.

AND DON'T FORGET THE CARROT!

"And there goes Lucky . . ." This is the announcer's familiar line at the dog track at the start of the race. Lucky refers to a stuffed rabbit that moves around the track just in front of the lead dog, an incentive that keeps all the dogs running faster. Liars are a lot like dogs. They need an incentive to confess. And an incentive is much more powerful if it's offered in a specific way. The payoff for confessing needs to be immediate, clear, specific, and compelling. You can't just tell a person what he'll gain by being truthful or lose by continuing to lie; you must make it real for him—so real, in fact, that he can feel, taste, touch, see, and hear it. Make it his reality. Let him experience fully the pleasure of being honest and the pain of continuing the lie. Involve as many of the senses as you can, particularly visual, auditory, and kinesthetic. Create images for the person to see, sounds for him to hear, and sensations that he can almost feel. You want to make this experience as real as possible.

The best way to do it is to first state the positives, then state the negatives, and then present the choice. You want to use this type of imagery with the silver bullets.

For example, suppose you are a boss investigating the

possibility that your employee is embezzling money from the company. Here's how you might talk to him: "Bill, you need to tell me the whole story* so we can put this behind us. Look, I've got big plans for you. You know that corner office with the green marble floors and mirrored bar? Well, pretty soon you'll be sitting behind that solid oak desk and running your own division. Of course you'll have your own assistant—probably Cathy. And when you drive to work each morning you'll be able to park in one of the reserved spaces. The monthly executive dinner meetings as well as use of the company vacation home in Hawaii will be yours as well."

Do you see how imagery helped Bill imagine himself in his new position? His "logical" promotion has been transformed into an emotional experience.

Now you, as Bill's boss, pause, sigh, and in your best parental tone finish your statement. "Unfortunately, none of this will ever be possible if we don't clear the air about the missing money. Taking it is one thing—we all make mistakes. I have, you have, we all have. But I can't have a liar working here. If you wait for accounting to tell me, as tough as it will be for me to do, you'll be out of here real fast. And unfortunately you know how these things can get

---

*The phrase "whole story" is more effective than asking someone to confess or tell the truth. By asking for the whole story you're not implying that he's been lying to you and you're giving him credit for being partially honest. Now he just has to go a little further and be completely honest. Asking someone to tell the truth is asking him to reverse his original position, the lie. And this is more difficult to bring about.

around. Getting another job will be very difficult for you. As you pound the pavement each day looking for work you'll find one door after another slamming shut in front of you. I sure wouldn't want to face your wife every night when you tell her that you had no luck finding a new job. So what's it going to be? The corner office and the bright future, or the disgrace and pain of losing everything?"

Above all, be consistent

Keep your message consistent. Remember that we all communicate on two levels: verbal and nonverbal. For instance, when you give an ultimatum, make sure that your nonverbal communication is consistent with your words. If you tell someone that you have "had enough and are through being lied to" only to remain where you are, you're not going to be very convincing. In this instance you would need to get up and walk toward the exit. You can always come back with another strategy later. Your behavior must always reflect the intensity and passion of your message.

Quick Tip: Always use the person's name when you're speaking. People tend to listen more closely and respond more compliantly when they hear their name.

If You Think That's Bad, Wait Until You Hear This!

This bullet works well because it forces the liar into thinking emotionally instead of logically. It alleviates his guilt by making him feel that he's not alone, and it throws him off by creating a little anger and/or curiosity. Plus he thinks that you and he are exchanging information, instead of his giving you something for nothing.

Sample question formation: "The reason I'm asking you these questions is that I've done some things that I'm not too proud of, either. I can understand why you might have . . . In a way I'm almost relieved. Now I don't feel too bad." At this point he will ask you to get more specific about your actions. But insist that he tell you first. Hold out and he'll come clean.

It Was an Accident. Really!

This is a great strategy because it makes him feel that it would be a good thing to have you know exactly what happened. He did something wrong, true, but that is no longer your concern. You shift the focus of your concern to his intentions, not his actions. This makes it easy for him to confess to his behavior and "make it okay" with the explanation that it was unintentional. He feels that you care about his motivation. In other words, you let him know that the source of your concern is not *what* he's done, but *why* he's done it.

Sample question formation: "I can understand that maybe you didn't plan on its happening. Things just got out of control and you acted without thinking. I'm fine with that—an accident, right? But if you did this on purpose, I don't think that I could ever forgive you. You need to tell me that you didn't do it intentionally. Please."

The Boomerang

Firing this bullet really throws a psychological curveball. With this example you tell him that he did something good, not bad. He's completely thrown off by this.

Scenario A

You suspect that Richard is stealing from the company. You want to find out if this is true, and if so, how long it's been going on.

Sample question formation: "Hey, Richard, I think you and I can become very wealthy partners. It seems that you've been cutting in on my action a little bit. But that's okay. We can work together, you old devil." You want to seem glad that you know what he's doing.

Scenario B

You suspect that your spouse may be having an affair.

Sample question formation: "You know, John, while I'm not thrilled about what was going on behind my back [this phrase is said to gain credibility; starting off with an honest statement makes what follows more believable], you should have said something. I could have saved you a lot of sneaking around. Maybe all three of us could get together. It might be fun. All this sneaking around is silly."

Wow, he's blown away. He has an incentive for telling the truth that's better than what he was doing on the sly. In other words, he thinks that by coming clean, he'll have more fun doing what he's been doing. If he's not cheating on you, he'll think you're nuts, but you will nonetheless have the truth.

Scenario C

You want to see if your interviewee has lied on her résumé.

Sample question formation: "As we both know, everybody pads his résumé just a bit. Personally, I think it shows guts. It tells me that the person isn't afraid to take on new responsibilities. Which parts were you most creative with on this résumé?"

Truth or Consequences

With this bullet you force your antagonist to work with you or you both end up with nothing. This is the exact opposite of the boomerang. Here the person has nothing unless he cooperates with you. Since you have nothing anyway (meaning you don't have the truth), it's a good tradeoff for you. The following parable illustrates this point nicely.

A greedy and evil watermelon farmer realizes that someone has been stealing one watermelon from him each night. Try as he might, he cannot catch the thief. Frustrated and annoyed, one afternoon he goes into his vast watermelon patch and injects one of the melons with a lethal poison. Not to be totally cruel, he posts a sign that reads, "To the person who is stealing from me: I have poisoned one of the watermelons. Steal from me, and you will be risking your life." The next morning he goes out, and while he is pleased to see that the thief has not struck, he finds a note left for him. "Dear Farmer: Tonight I too have poisoned one of your watermelons. Now we can either work together or they will all rot."

Scenario A

You suspect that your housekeeper has stolen from you.

Sample question formation: "I'd rather hear it from you first. I can live with what you did/what happened, but not with your lying to me about it. If you don't tell me, then it's over. If you tell me the truth, things can go back to how they were. But if you don't, then we have no chance here, and you'll have nothing."

You can't let the person benefit from his action unless he tells you about it. Now the only way he can set things straight is by confessing and cooperating with you.

This bullet allows him to confess to his wrongdoing with less anxiety. You want to convey that anything that he's done pales in comparison to his lying to about it: "Doing what you did is one thing—we can get past that—but lying about it is something that I cannot deal with. Just be honest and we'll be able to put this whole thing behind us. Until you come clean, it won't be possible for you to continue here."

Speak Now or Forever Hold Your Peace

Plumbers know that the time to negotiate a price is when the basement is flooded. Obviously, the motivation for the homeowner to act is highest when the problem is most intense. And when might the pilots' union go on strike? Right before holidays, the peak days of the year for airline travel. The name of the game is leverage.

Deadlines produce results. How fast do you think you would get your taxes in if there was no deadline? Or if there was a deadline but no penalty was attached to it? How fast would you get a project done at work if your boss told you that the results had to be on his desk before you retired? Would you ever get around to using those coupons if they had no expiration date? We have deadlines with penalties attached in almost every area of our life.

Human beings place a premium on that which is scarce. Simply put, rare equals good. You can dramatically increase your leverage by conveying that this is the only time that you will discuss this. Let him know that (a) this is his last chance he'll have for explaining himself, and (b) you can get what you need from someone else. Try increasing the rate of your speech as well. The faster you speak, the less time he has to process the information, and it conveys a stronger sense of urgency.

Give a deadline with a penalty for not meeting it. Deadlines force action. If the guilty party thinks that he can always come clean, then he will take a wait-and-see approach before tipping his hand. Let the person know that you already know and have proof of his action. And admitting his sins now will give him the opportunity to explain his side.

Sample question formation I: "I want to hear it from you now. After tomorrow, anything you say won't make a difference to me."

Sample question formation II: "I know what happened/ what you did. I was hoping I would hear it from you first. It would mean a lot to me to hear your side of it. I know there are two sides to every story, and before I decide what to do, I want to hear yours."

Hearing this gives him the feeling he still has a chance if

he confesses. After all, what really happened can't be as bad as what you heard. Confessing now is a way of cutting his losses.

Reverse Course

This sequence provides the person with an unforeseen and unexpected incentive to tell the truth. You convey to him that what happened or what he did was a good thing insofar as it allows you and he to establish an even better relationship—personal or professional. You give him an opportunity to explain why he took that choice. You also blame yourself. Here's how it works.

Sample question formation: "I understand why you would have done that. Clearly you wouldn't have unless you had a good reason. You were probably treated unfairly or something was lacking. What can I do to help so that it doesn't happen again?" This is an assumptive question— you take for granted you are right in your assertion that he acted in this way. When he begins to tell you his grievances, it paves the way for him to justify his previous actions—his misdeeds—to you. Keep interjecting the following phrases: "I take full responsibility for your actions. Let's work together to see how we can avoid this happening again. I understand completely. You were right to do what you did."

I Hate to Do This,
But You Leave Me No Choice

This is the only strategy that involves threat. The other bullets make it comfortable for the person to reveal his true self. This one turns up the heat a little. You let him become aware that there are going to be greater ramifications and repercussions than just lying to you—things that he never thought about.

In this bullet you up the ante, but you rely on his imagination to set the terms of the damage that you can inflict. His mind will race through every possible scenario as his own fears turn against him. You create a larger problem and then offer a solution. The deceiver made his choice to deceive based upon a gain/loss ratio that he deemed to be to his benefit. Letting him know that the ramifications are much greater than he ever considered helps to reestablish the risk/reward ratio in your favor.

Sample question formation I: "I didn't want to have to do this, but you leave me no choice." This will inevitably propel him to respond: "Do what?" At this point he's waiting to see what the tradeoff will be. But do not commit yourself to an action. Let him create in his own mind scenarios of what you will do unless he confesses.

Sample question formation II: "You know what I can do, and I'll do it. If you don't want to tell me now, don't. I'll just do what I have to do."

After this statement pay close attention to his response. If he focuses on what you will do to him, the odds lean more toward guilty. However, if he reasserts that he's done nothing, he may in fact be innocent of your accusation. This is because the guilty person needs to know the penalty to determine if it makes sense for him to stick to his story. Only the guilty have the option of confessing. They are the ones who have to make a decision. The innocent has no such choice to make, and therefore nothing to consider.

I Guess You're Not Allowed

Never underestimate the power of appealing to a person's ego. Sometimes you want to inflate it, and other times you want to attack it. And as you may have guessed, this bullet is for attacking.

It's truly saddening how fragile some people's egos are—but for these people this bullet works very well. It really gets under their skin. A friend of mine who is a police detective loves this technique. The following is a generic example of how it is used.

"We picked up this guy for beating up on a couple of homeless guys. We were getting absolutely nowhere with him. Finally, after half an hour, we were thinking we had to let him walk. We had no case because one of the homeless men disappeared and the other was too afraid. So I looked at this jackass and said, 'Oh, okay, I get it. You're afraid that Niko [a drug runner he has worked with before] is gonna kick the crap out of you. That's it, isn't it? You can't go to court over this because he owns you. You're his little slave." After the suspect hurled a few expletives he shouted, "Nobody owns me." He became indignant. And to prove his point, he did what he had to: he confessed, proudly.

Sample question formation I: "I think I know what it is—you're not allowed to tell me. Somebody else is pulling the strings and you'll get in trouble."

Sample question formation II: "Okay, I think I know what it is. You'd tell me the truth if you could, but you don't have the power to. You're not able to and you probably feel as bad as I do about it."

Higher Authority

If the situation is right, this bullet will work exceptionally well. An acquaintance of mine who works in the human resources department of a large financial firm loves this one. She tells me that it's her greatest tool for weeding out undesirable candidates for employment.

As long as the person believes that you are on his side, he'll take the bait. All you have to do is let him know that anything he's lied about can now be cleared up in seconds. However, if anyone else finds out about it later, it's too late.

Scenario A

You think an interviewee has lied on his résumé.

Sample question formation: "I'm going to do something nice for you because I think you'd be great for this job. They're going to want to verify everything on the résumé. Even the slightest exaggeration will prevent you from being hired. So let's clean it up now. What specifically needs to be revised so that it's perfectly accurate?"

Scenario B

You want to know if your secretary leaves early when you're out of the office.

Sample question formation: "The vice president from corporate is coming in today. He's asked about your hours, so I'm going to tell him that you come in early on the days that you leave early. Do you remember what days last month you finished up early and took off?"

Do you see how disarming this is? You're not yelling at her or demanding answers. It's us against them, and you're here to help. Plus the phrase "finished up early" implies that she's done all her work—and efficiently at that. You're on her side, and you're going to work together to smooth things over.

The Great Unknown

For most people it is next to impossible to see anything or understand any concept by itself. This means that when a new situation arises we have an inherent need to compare and contrast it with something familiar. But what if there was no category for it fall into? This can be a very frightening experience.

If you want the truth and the penalty for lying is clear, then the suspect knows the up side and the down side for confessing and he can weigh his options. It stands to reason that in instances where the penalty for lying is not severe enough, you will have difficulty getting the truth. So you need to remove the penalty from the *known* and put it where it's uncomfortable: *the unknown.*

You can obtain maximum leverage by explaining how the ramifications of his deceit will be something that the suspect has never known before. Even if he believes that you are limited in what you can do to him and in what the penalty will be, the severity of the penalty can be manipulated in two major ways to make it appear much more severe. The two factors are time and impact.

Time: Give no indication of when the penalty will occur. When things happen unexpectedly, the degree of anguish is more potent. If he knows he won't get a chance to mentally prepare and brace himself, the anxiety is greatly heightened.

Impact: Convey that his entire life will be disrupted and

drastically altered for the worse. He needs to see that this event is not isolated and will instead have a ripple effect. When bad things happen we are often comforted in knowing that it will soon be over and the rest of our life will remain intact and unaffected. But if these things are not assured, we become increasingly fearful and concerned.

Scenario

You suspect an employee of stealing. You can threaten to fire him, in which case he may weigh his options and decide that you may never find out the truth. However, if you said . . .

Sample question formation: "Smith, at any time should I discover that you've been lying to me about this, I will have your desk cleaned out and security escort you to your car. There will be no good-byes. I'll march you right out of here in the middle of the day. And this is a small business community—try getting a job with this hanging over your head. You'll be completely through."

You then ask him to come clean now and offer him the option of a transfer to another part of the company so you can both put this behind you. This last sentence is called an easy-out clause and is talked about more in part 6.

I Couldn't Care Less

A primary law governing human nature is that we all have a need to feel significant. Nobody wants to be thought of as unimportant, or feel that his ideas and thinking is irrelevant. Take away a person's belief that he has value and he'll do just about anything to reassert his sense of importance. If he feels that you don't care that he's lying to you, he will want to know—better, he needs to know—why you're so cavalier and dispassionate. Did you expect something like this from him? Do you know something that he doesn't? Are you uninterested in his opinion or feelings for you? Do you plan on seeking retribution or revenge? When you show emotion, you show that you care. Your apathy toward the situation will unnerve him immensely. He will begin to crave recognition and acceptance, in any form. He needs to know you care what happens, and if talking about his misdeeds is the only way he can find out, he will. Some examples of what you can say are as follows:

Sample question formation A: "I know and I just don't care. This is not for me."

Sample question formation B: "I've got other things to think about. Maybe we'll talk some other time."

Sample question formation C: "You do what you have to do, that's fine with me."

When you ignore a person you usually do not make eye contact. However, in this situation, you want to make an instant impact, and engaging him in direct eye contact does this best. To make this even more powerful, stare at him. In our culture, as in most, staring is often dehumanizing. We stare at things that are on display, such as caged animals. When you stare at someone he often feels less significant and will seek to reassert his value.

These attack sequences should do the job quite nicely. However, if you're still not getting the answers you want, it's time for the advanced techniques in part 5. Remember to read this section through carefully before using any of these techniques.

TACTICS FOR DETECTING DECEIT AND GATHERING INFORMATION IN CASUAL CONVERSATIONS

"Truth is the first casualty of civil discourse."
—DAVID J. LIEBERMAN

Now what about those times when you're not quite sure if someone is lying to you, but a full-fledged interrogation is out of the question? Here are some excellent ways to gather more information without being obvious.

GENERAL CONVERSATIONS

1. Ask-a-Fact

During the conversation simply ask general, clear questions pertaining to your suspicion. This causes the person you are questioning to recall information. If he spoke the truth, then he will answer you quickly and effortlessly. If he was lying, your clues to deceit will let you know. Most important, note how long it takes him to call up the information. If he's lying, he'll take a while to answer because he first has check his response mentally to be sure it makes sense. Made-up stories do not have details because they never happened!

Ask questions that will give you an objective, not a subjective, response. For instance, if you think an employee was home when he said he would be away on vacation, don't ask him how he enjoyed the weather in Florida. People generally take longer to respond to these type of questions. Instead, ask one such as "Did you rent a car?" Casually ask more questions in the same vein. Once he answers yes to any question, ask for more detail. If he's lying, he'll try to keep the facts straight and will take his time answering further questions. People love to talk about themselves. The only way that someone would want to change the subject is if he's uncomfortable with the questions. If you're asking simple, innocuous questions you should expect that he would want to extend the conversation, not end it. Most people will love to go on endlessly about the new restaurant they went to, the trip they took or the job they turned down . . . unless of course they're lying and you keep asking questions.

2. Add-a-False Fact

In this sequence you add a fact and ask the person to comment on it. This fact is one that you've made up, but one that sounds perfectly reasonable. For instance, let's say that while you are at a party someone proclaims that he has just returned from an East African safari. You could tell him that you heard that East Africa had had record hot temperatures. This is a fact that he might be able to confirm or deny regardless of whether he had actually been there. Furthermore, he could just plead ignorance of the fact and proclaim that it was very, very hot. Either way you're unable to detect deceit.

Here's how you can detect it. You can mention that your uncle who works as a customs officer at the Nairobi airport told you that everyone going to Africa was given special instructions on how to avoid malaria. As soon as he validates your claim in an attempt to back up his assertion that he has gone to Africa, you know that his story is untrue. Otherwise he would simply say that he doesn't know what your uncle is talking about.

Here are the criteria:

a. Your statement has to be untrue. If he merely confirms something that's actually true, you haven't learned anything new.

b. It has to sound reasonable. Otherwise the person you are questioning might think it's a joke.

c. Your assertion has to be something that would directly affect the person, so he would have firsthand knowledge of this "fact." In other words, in the above scenario you wouldn't say you heard that the tilt of the earth's axis made for exceptional viewing of the night sky.

3. Support-a-Fact

In this sequence you take what the person says and request proof, but in a very nonthreatening manner. For example, in the case of the person who claimed he had gone on safari, you might let him know that you would love to see pictures of the trip. If he offers up a reason why you can't see the pictures—didn't take any, didn't come out right, left lens cap on—then this should arouse some suspicion.

Let's say you're a talk-show producer and you want to check the credibility of a guest. You might say, "Your story about this government conspiracy is fascinating. Since you worked in the building, it would be great if you would show us your security access card."

4. Expand-a-Fact

Use this clue to determine how far someone is willing to go to get what she wants. All you do is expand on a fact that she has already offered. If she just goes on without correcting you, then you know that she may be lying about what she's said so far and/or is willing to lie to get you to see her point. Let's say that you and your friend are deciding on what movie to see. You suggest *Lost in Paradise*, but your friend, who doesn't want to see this, offers as evidence a coworker who has already seen it and didn't like it. You then say, "Oh, well, if no one in your office liked it, I guess it's probably no good." If she lets it go at that—not correcting your false assertion—then you know that she either lied initially about her coworker or will lie in this situation.

Let's take another example. Your secretary asks you for the rest of the day off because she's not feeling well. You might say, "Oh, of course, if you've got a fever and a bad headache, by all means take off." She never claimed to have these symptoms. You merely expanded on her statement. Again, if she does not correct you, she is clearly either lying about being ill or willing to agree to anything to go home. Of course she may simply be sick and eager to get home. However, her not correcting your statement indicates that she does not mind being deceitful to get what she wants.

SPECIAL OCCASIONS

These strategies are used when a person is reluctant to reveal information for unselfish reasons. Or the situation is such that you have to be very delicate in your approach. These people are coming from a different psychological position, so the situation must be addressed

uniquely. The strategies usually fall into one of the following
ten categories.

Third-Party Protection

This tactic is a little different in that it is used if someone is
reluctant to tell you something that involves another person.
You have appeal to his ego and let him forget that he's telling tales out of school.

Scenario A

Your attorney is telling you about a case that a fellow attorney screwed up on. Simply asking, "What did he do
wrong?" would probably get you nowhere. However, by
turning it around you create an incentive for him to tell you.

Sample question formation: "Had you handled the case,
what would you have done differently?" This magic phrase
opens the floodgates of conversation.

Scenario B

While chatting with Brad, one of your salespeople, you
would like to find out why Susan's sales figures are low. But
simply asking him why she's not doing well might prove
fruitless. Out of loyalty to her, he may be reluctant to say

NEVER BE LIED TO AGAIN

anything. So you turn the question around and he becomes completely forthcoming.

Sample question formation: "What areas do you think Susan can improve in?"

In both of these scenarios the conversation is positive. The other person feels as if he's doing a good thing by answering your question. And in fact he is. Had you asked it the other way around, you would likely have met with great reluctance to speak.

2

The Power Play

Sometimes the person reluctant to tell the truth is in a position of power. In these situations it's usually inappropriate and futile to become argumentative. In these instances you want to bring the conversation to a personal level. Here are two examples of how this is done.

Scenario A

You're trying to sell to a buyer who doesn't want to buy and is not giving you a reason that you truly believe. Your objective will be to get to the real objection.

Sample question formation: "I do this for a living. My family relies on me to support them. Clearly we have a fine product and you're a reasonable man. Would you mind telling me what I did to offend you?"

Now your buyer is caught off guard and will undoubtedly follow with "Oh, you didn't offend me. It's just that . . ."

Offend is a powerful word. Now you'll get the real objection because he figures that telling you the truth is the only way to show you that you haven't offended him.

Scenario B

Your boss is reluctant to tell you exactly why you were passed up for the promotion.

Sample question formation: "Ms. Smith, I understand where you're coming from, and I respect your thoughts. Someday I hope to be as successful in this company as you are today. Let me ask you one question, if I may? If you were me, sitting in this chair now, do you think that you would have a better chance of moving up in the company if you were aware of your shortcomings?"

3

Hurt Feelings

In this situation someone is lying to you to protect your feelings—perhaps one of those little white lies. You're interested in getting at the truth. A touch of guilt makes the other person reevaluate his approach.

Scenario

You feel that the truth is being withheld from you for your own benefit.

Sample question formation I: "I know you don't want to offend me, but you're hurting me more by not being perfectly honest." Using the word *perfectly* here serves a purpose. It gives the person credit for being partially honest with you.

Sample question formation II: "If you don't tell me, no one else will. If I can't count on you for this, I don't know what I would do."

4

It's a Matter of Opinion

Trying to detect deceit in a person's opinion is hard. You can't exactly call someone a liar, arguing that she doesn't really believe what she is saying to be the truth. The following is an excellent method for revealing a person's true feelings in any situation.

Scenario A

You're not sure if your boss really likes your idea for a new advertising campaign, even though she says she does.

Sample question sequence I:
"Do you *like* the concept for my new idea?"
"Sure. It's very original."
"Well, what would it take for you to *love* the idea?"

In this example your boss has committed to liking the idea. You don't argue with her or press her on it. The words you use in your response indicate that you know there is room for improvement. She feels comfortable offering criticism because she feels that you expect her to do so.

Scenario B

You want to know if your son is looking forward to going to camp this summer.
Sample question sequence II:
"Are you *excited* about camp next month?"
"Yeah. It'll be fun."
"What would it take for you to be *really* excited about going?"

Again, he feels comfortable answering honestly because your questions to him make it obvious that you know that everything's not perfect.

5

I Don't Know

Most people don't like to be wrong. Furthermore, most people don't like to be put in a situation where they feel they have to defend themselves. As a result, oftentimes when you ask someone what she is thinking or how she feels, she replies, "I don't know." This response can stall a conversation and leave you searching for answers. Sometimes it's just easier to say "I don't know," which is often why we say it in the first place. Either way, when you hear "I don't know," try some of the following responses:

1. "Okay, then why don't you tell me how you've come to think the way you do?"
2. "I know you don't know, but if you were to guess, what do you think it might be?"
3. "Can you tell me what part of this you're okay with?"
4. "In what past situations have you felt similar to this one?"
5. "What emotion best describes what you're thinking right now?"
6. "Can you think of just one reason?"
7. "What one word comes closest to describing what you're thinking?"

In all of these responses, you're taking the pressure off. You acknowledge the person's difficulty in answering. You then seem to be asking her to provide something else, when in reality your new question is aimed at getting your initial question answered.

"I don't know" could also mean that the person feels guilty or foolish about her actions. In this case you want to relieve her of the responsibility. This is done in the following way:

Sample question formation: "I know you're not sure about why you did that, so can you think of any unconscious motivations that may have been at work?" This works well because she doesn't have to feel responsible for her actions. It was not her "intention" to do what she did. Her behavior was not consciously motivated.

6

I'm Simply Embarrassed

In this encounter someone is unwilling to tell you the truth or may lie to you out of embarrassment. The usual tactics don't work here because the person probably isn't obligated to tell you and more than likely will have nothing to gain by doing so. Therefore you need to create an incentive for telling the truth in an environment that makes him feel comfortable.

Scenario A

Your son doesn't want to tell you about the bully who took his lunch money.

Sample question formation: "It's okay if you don't want to talk about it. [This is a key phrase because it instantly disarms the other person. It lets them know that he's not going to get verbally beaten up.] When I was your age the same thing happened to me. And after I learned what to say to him, he never bothered me again. Would you like to hear what you can do?"

Scenario B

As a physician you're speaking with a patient who is reluctant to discuss her previous sexual relationships.

Sample question formation: "I understand your hesitancy, and if you would prefer not to discuss it, then we won't. Whenever I have a patient who feels uncomfortable I do it this way and it's much easier and quicker. I'm going to ask you simple yes-or-no questions and you respond accordingly."

This works well because the patient knows that there won't be an embarrassing discussion or elaboration of anything she says. The yes-or-no format can be used with just about anyone in any situation that makes one uncomfortable revealing personal information.

Scenario C

You want to find out if the foreman of your construction crew has been thinking of leaving your company.

Sample question formation: "Mike, on a scale from one to ten, where one means you've only thought about looking for other work and ten means you're very interested in going with another company, where might you fit in?"

Three important criteria need to be kept in mind. First, notice that you don't say "where do you fall?" as it is typically phrased. The word *fall* is downward and negative. It puts his focus lower on the number line. "Fit in" directs his thinking between two numbers and is positive. Second, the word *might* is used to cushion his association to his answer, helping him to feel less attached to it.

Finally, notice too, that you don't say on a scale from one to ten where one is *no interest*. You allowed him to answer with the "easiest option" offered. If in fact, he had no interest whatsoever, then he would go outside the perameters of your question and be free to tell you just that.

Scenario D

You think the new intern mixed up two piles of papers and shredded the documents that were supposed to be copied.

Sample question formation: "Nelson, if you're the one who did this, it's all right. I remember when I first started here. What I'm going to tell you is between you and me, okay? Good. I once made copies of a confidential memo instead of the lunch menu and placed a copy in each person's mailbox."

The best way to get someone to confide in you is for you to confide in him. This instantly puts the other person at ease. It shows that you trust him, and he also feels obligated to share with you something he's done that he feels uncomfortable with.

7

Divide and Conquer

This is a situation where there are two or more people from whom you can get the truth. The mistake that most of us make is to say something like "Come on, guys. Somebody tell me what's going here!" We find ourselves sounding a lot like *M*A*S*H*'s Frank Burns—looking for cooperation everywhere and finding it nowhere. This plea is often ineffective because of a psychological phenomenon known as social responsibility.

Have you ever heard somebody scream from an apartment window? While most of us have been in such a situation, we don't feel any strong inclination to do anything about it. It's not because we're cold and uncaring. It's because the social responsibility to act is divided among many people. Everyone assumes that if it's an emergency, somebody else has already called the police. There have been countless stories of a person's having a heart attack on a crowded street while people just walked by. Nobody does anything because they assume somebody else will; alternatively, they think that since nobody else is doing anything, the person must be okay.

When there is a diffusion of responsibility, the impetus to act just isn't there. If you want answers or if you want

132

somebody to do something, you have to increase his responsibility. This is best accomplished by appealing to one person at a time. If you get nowhere with the first person, go to the next and appeal to him.

Scenario A

Several of your sorority sisters pulled a practical joke and you want to find out who is responsible.

Sample question formation I: "Eileen, I'm coming to you for one reason and one reason only. I know I can trust you to tell me the truth. You can trust me like I can trust you. You're not like they are. I know I can count on you to do the right thing." If you don't get anywhere with her, go to the next person with the same speech. Somebody will crack.

Sample question formation II: "Jennifer, who did this is not important. I don't even care. What is, is our friendship. I want to know that I can trust you. I think I can, but I need for you to speak honestly with me. It's not that I'm so concerned with who did it—only that you are truthful with me about it." If you don't get anywhere with her, go to someone else with the same speech.

8

Professional Reliance

From attorneys and plumbers to mechanics and teachers, we rely on professionals to be honest and fair. And while most are, there are a few who are not.

These situations can be tough because you don't have the specific knowledge and expertise to ask the right questions. Unfortunately the less-than-reputable professional is all too aware of this. And while your clues to deception will let you know what kind of person you're dealing with, the following strategy will prove useful in these situations.

1. Always, if possible, get a second opinion. It's easy to do and can save you a lot of heartache.
2. Make sure the person is licensed, insured, and registered to do the actual work.
3. Have your agreement drawn up in writing. Oral contracts aren't worth the paper they're written on.
4. Ask for referrals or testimonials.

If he balks at any one of these points, you might want to take your business elsewhere. The con artist operates best when you're in the dark.

Finally, the following strategy should give you an accurate insight into the person's intentions. The key is to ask for the opposite of what you really want.

Scenario A

Let's say that your travel agent suggests the Five-Day Cruise Getaway vacation package for you. You're looking to really let loose; you want a trip that will be nonstop fun. But you're not sure if she's pushing this package for the commission or if she really believes that it's a great deal.

Sample question formation: "The brochure looks great, Sandy. I just want to make sure that this is not one of those party boats. I'm looking for some rest and relaxation. Is this that kind of trip?"

By asking your question this way, you will know the intentions of your travel agent and the answer to your question. If she answers yes, than you know that the cruise is not for you or she is lying to get your business. Either way you are not going to book this cruise through her. Only by telling you what she thinks you don't want to hear will she establish herself as honest, and you'll have confirmed that this is the cruise you want to go on.

Scenario B

You asked your waiter for decaffeinated coffee and five minutes later the busboy comes by with a filled cup of coffee.

Sample question formation: "This is regular coffee, right?" If he confirms that it is, either he doesn't care enough to know for sure or it really is regular. Again, either way, you now know that you may not be getting what you asked for. However, should he tell you that it is decaffeinated—something he thinks you don't want—then you can be pretty sure that you're getting what you originally asked for.

9

I Don't Know and I Don't Care

Few things are more frustrating than dealing with someone who just doesn't give a damn. Why? Because you don't have a whole lot to work with. You've got zero leverage. He's got nothing at risk, so you've got little bargaining power. Here's how to get some. You simply have to change the equation so he's got something at stake. This technique is the ultimate apathy buster.

Scenario A

You take your car to the mechanic and he tells you it will be fixed by Friday. But you just know that something's going to come up and it will be sitting in his garage all weekend.

Sample question formation: "Okay, Joe. Tomorrow's fine. Just so you know, my wife is pregnant and she's due any day. That's our only car, so if you can think of any reason why it may not be ready by Friday, you've got to let me know now."

Scenario B

You ask the waiter if there is MSG, an additive that some people are allergic to, in the salad and he tells you there isn't. He doesn't seems terribly convincing and you just want to make sure.

Sample question formation: "Okay, Albert, that's great. Just so you know I'm deathly allergic to MSG. One forkful and it's off to the hospital I go." After hearing this, do you think Albert may want to double-check with the chef?

Notice that the equation changes in these two scenarios. Initially neither the mechanic nor the waiter is terribly concerned about your schedule or what you're eating. However, their apathy quickly gives way to concern because now they're dealing with more than just an inconvenience. Simply change the stakes and the leverage is yours.

10

I Just Heard

Most people who lie usually confide in at least one other person. Getting the truth from this person can be done easily, if it's done right. It's important to let this person believe that you already know the truth and then add your emotional reaction to it. Adding an emotion makes you appear genuine because the fact that you know the truth is overshadowed by your reaction to it. Simply use an emotion that best fits the situation, such as sympathy, surprise, fear, joy, concern, humor, and so on.

Let's take a look at a couple of general statements that would be said to the person whom you believe knows the truth:

1. Sympathy: "I can't believe what Sam did. I am truly very, very sorry. If there's anything I can do for you or whatever, please just let me know, okay?"
2. Concern: "I just found out; how dare they do that to Kim? I've got a good mind to go down there myself and give them hell. How are you holding up through all this?"
3. Humor: "Mary, is Joe a magnet for odd things or what? He just told me and I still can't believe it."

Make sure you act as if your suspicion is true and let this person assume that you already have knowledge of it. Then offer the appropriate emotional response and you have maximum credibility.

DIRECTING THE CONVERSATION

You can steer a conversation in any direction that you choose. Take this example. Let's say that while you are at a friend's house, she shows you her brand-new dining room table. If you want to know if it was really expensive, would asking directly be your best bet? Usually not, because she may get a little defensive. But if you said to your friend that it's the most gorgeous table you have ever seen, what might she respond with? You guessed it—how expensive it was! If you said, "This looks like it cost a fortune. How could you spend so much on a table?" what response might you get? She would tell you about its quality and the crafts-manship that went into it. When you say it's expensive, she'll talk about the quality. If you say that it looks beau-tiful, she'll tell you about the cost. By asking the right ques-tions you can steer the conversation in any direction you want and elicit the information that you need.

You can also control the mode of the response as well. Have you ever noticed the ritual that takes place when you pass someone in the hall or on the elevator? You smile, she smiles. You smile and nod, she smiles and nods. You give a hello, and then she will usually speak as well. The one who responds to the situation first is the one who controls the mode of the exchange.

The same goes for the pace of a conversation. Try this on your own. Ask someone an open-ended question—a question that cannot be answered with a simple yes or no— slowly and deliberately. Watch how the other person takes his time to respond. Then ask a question speaking quickly, and the answer is sure to be paced at a similar rate.

In order to best detect deceit you may want to guide the conversation in a particular direction. You can do this very efficiently with just a few well-chosen words. After he makes a statement, you can use the following key words to direct the flow of information in any way that you choose. They can be used to extract information from any conversation.

1. *Meaning* . . . Saying this word after he speaks directs his thinking and the conversation toward the larger picture, giving you a better look at his overall position. He will offer the reason for the position he's taken.

Example I

"I'm the highest-paid person at this institution."

"Meaning?"

"That I'm the only one with the experience and education to do this job. I've worked my way up the ladder over a fifteen-year period."

Example II

"I'm in charge of the entire operation."

"Meaning?"

"That the boss put me in charge when he left. If you've got any problems, you'll have to deal with me."

2. *And* . . . This one-word response gives you more lateral information. You'll be able to gather additional facts related to his position.

Example I

"I'm sorry, but that's the best we can do."

"And . . ."

"The offer is as it stands. We've looked at the pricing schedule and delivery options three times."

Example II

"I'm in charge of the entire operation."

"And . . ."

"That means everything—inventory, scheduling, and employee relations."

3. *So . . .* This response makes him get more specific, giving you the details of his position.

Example I

"I offer the best level of medical care you can get."

"So . . ."

"If you came to me, I'd give you a full blood workup and x-rays as just part of the standard check-up."

Example II

"Our company guarantees you job security."

"So . . ."

"If you ever had to take a leave of absence, your job would be here for you."

4. *Now . . .* This response makes him translate his position into a specific action. He will proceed to tell you exactly what he means and how it applies to you.

Example I

"Our policy is to stand behind our shareholders."

"Now . . ."

"You can either follow us or go out on your own. It's up to you."

Example II

"We offer the best guarantee in the business."

"Now . . ."

"You can sign here, and we'll get the paperwork going."

GETTING SPECIFIC

Sometimes you'll get an answer, but it doesn't do you much good. Here are some great ways for narrowing a vague response to give you a more direct, truthful answer. The two main areas regard thoughts and actions. The following responses show how to draw out a specific answer.

I. In Response to an Opinion or Belief

Example

"I don't think the meeting went very well."
"How come?" (broad response)
"I just don't, all right?!"

Some responses will produce a more productive response:
"Compared with what?"
"How poorly did it go?"

If you ask for clarification, the person feels more obligated to respond. Asking a broad question in response to a general statement just produces more of the same.

II. In Response to a Reluctance to Commit

Example A

"I don't know if I could."

"*What do you mean, you don't know?*" *(broad response)*
"*I just don't know, all right?*"

Example B

"*I don't know if I could.*"
"*Why can't you?*" *(broad response)*
"*I don't know. I just can't.*"

Some responses will produce a more productive response:
"*What, specifically, prevents you?*"
"*What would have to happen for you to be able to?*"
"*What would change if you did?*"

Do you see how specific responses narrow the answer? Use this technique whenever you want to clarify a broad or ambiguous answer.

LET THE TRUTH BE TOLD

What simple words work better than any others? These three do:

Because: We're programmed to accept an explanation as valid if it follows this word.

Let's: This word generates a group atmosphere and initiates the bandwagon effect. It's a positive word that creates action.

Try: This little word is a powerful motivator because it implies that you will be unsuccessful, so it instills a "what's the harm" mentality. We all love to *try* things. The following sentence uses all three words in a construction that makes absolutely no sense, yet seems like it should.

"Let's give it a try because if it doesn't work we can always go back to the way it was."

Clearly you haven't introduced any reason for the person to take action. Yet it seems to make sense just the same.

A person will get defensive only if he feels he's under attack, so why attack? Let's look at the benefits of using these words to get to the truth.

"Did you take five dollars from petty cash?"
"Why did you take five dollars from petty cash?"
"Stop taking money from petty cash!"

What do all these phrases have in common? They're all accusatory and likely to produce an automatic "I didn't do it" response. If you wanted to know if he took the money, simply say, "The money that we take from petty cash? Let's try to keep it fewer than ten dollars at a time, because it works out better that way." Do you see how kind this statement is? It's easier to get to the truth because no one feels like he has to defend himself.

Use these words—*because, let's,* and *try*—whenever you want to gain information without sounding accusatory or demanding.

TAKING CONTROL

Now you're fully equipped to get the truth from any situation or conversation. But you can't operate if you can't get a word in edgewise. If you're in a situation where you are unable to speak because the person keeps talking or interrupting, the following are some great ways to get the floor. These seventeen zingers will stun them into silence. Use whichever one(s) you feel are most appropriate for the situation. They play on two susceptible angles of human nature—ego and curiosity.

1. "You're a smart person; let me ask you a question."
2. "Let me get your opinion on something."
3. "May I be the first person in your presence to finish a sentence?"
4. "Don't show your ignorance by interrupting."
5. "I'm sorry if the facts conflict with your opinion, but I would like to know . . ."
6. "Maybe you can help me with something."
7. "I know that you would want me to ask you this."
8. "You're the only person who would know the answer to this."
9. "I hope this news doesn't upset you."
10. "Before you say anything else, answer this question."
11. "I want to give my full attention to what you're saying, so let me just get this out of the way."
12. "I hope this doesn't offend you, but . . ."
13. "I don't want you to miss this."

14. "This is the last time you'll hear this."
15. "Do you have a good memory? Great, then you won't forget this."
16. "I'm sorry if the middle of my sentence ran into the beginning of yours."
17. "Along those lines . . ." It's easy to change the conversation when you begin with the other person's last thoughts.

MIND GAMES

"I am different from Washington, I have a higher, grander
standard of principle. Washington could not tell a lie.
I can lie, but I won't."
—MARK TWAIN

This section gives you two very powerful tools. The first shows you how to avoid being lied to in the first place. In the second, you will learn how to find out a person's true intention in any situation.

A STRONG DEFENSE: AVOIDING THE LIE

As the saying goes, the best defense is a good offense. Once you've been lied to, you can easily get to the truth with the techniques that you've learned. However, the best time to deal with a lie is before it turns into one. Confused? This may help. The following is a technique for cutting a suspicion off at the pass before it turns into deception.

Method 1

This is the method you use when you want the truth as it relates to a person's previous behavior. Here is a possible scenario: a parent suspects that her twelve-year-old son is smoking cigarettes. The following approaches are listed in order from worst to best.

a. "Have you been smoking cigarettes? I'm gonna kill you if I find out you have." This approach is awful, but unfortunately it is the most common. In her anger, the boy's mother links confessing to the truth with punishment. This destroys any incentive to confess. She is likely to be lied to.

b. "You've been smoking, haven't you?" This approach is a little better because the mother indicates that she has some type of proof or evidence. Such an approach will work sometimes. The child may not want to add lying to his already reprehensible act of smoking.

c. "I want to speak to you about your smoking." This is what I call an forward assumptive approach. The child feels that the parent already knows he is smoking. The focus of the request is on discussing it. The parent may get a response such as "I don't want to talk about it." However, the truth is revealed in that statement.

d. "I know all about the smoking and the sneaking around. You know I'm not happy about that, but I just want you to promise me that you won't drink alcohol until you're twenty-one."

This is by far the finest approach because it works on so many levels. First, it takes a forward assumptive stance— the parent "knows all about the smoking." Second, it uses two truisms (see part 5). The phrases "sneaking around" and "you know I'm not happy about that" set the tone for honesty. The child hears two things that he knows to be true: He was sneaking around and his mother is unhappy about his smoking. He is therefore willing to accept at face value what follows. Third, the mother gives her son an easy out. All he has to do is promise not to drink and he's home free. There's no threat or punishment, just honest statements followed by a deal that he believes to be true as well.

The guidelines to keep in mind for this procedure are as follows:

1. Assume your suspicion as fact.
2. State at least two truisms (facts that you both know to be true).
3. Switch the focus from a threat to a request.
4. The request should be easy for him to accept and sound reasonable.

Method 2

This method is used when you want the truth as it relates to a new decision. It is a simple but highly effective strategy to avoid being deceived. Oftentimes someone wants to tell us the truth, but it's easier to tell a lie instead. The person knows the answer you want to hear and will give it to you whether he believes it or not.

However, if he doesn't know what you want, then he won't be able to deceive you. Read the following examples and notice how well the second phrasing masks your true question.

- "We're restructuring some positions. How would you like to work directly under me in finance?" Or "We're moving some people around. Would you prefer to get more experience in finance or marketing?"
- "Would you like me to cook for you tonight?" Or "Do you feel like eating in or out tonight?"

- "I'm thinking of asking Rhonda out. What do you think of her?" Or "What do you think of Rhonda?"

To use this technique, just make sure that when you phrase the question you mask your preference, and the respondent will give you an honest answer.

KNOW THY ENEMY: KNOWING THE LIAR AND HIS INTENTIONS

The following example illustrates a process that is becoming very popular in employee screening tests. The questions below are asked the prospective employee to determine if he is an honest person. If you really wanted the job, how would you answer these questions?

Have you ever stolen anything in your life?
Have you ever run a red light?
Do you have a friend who has ever shoplifted?
Have you ever had thoughts of killing someone?

Many of us would have to answer yes to most of these questions. And that is precisely the answer a prospective employee is looking for. Why? Because the honest answer is yes for most of us—saints excluded. The employer's task is finding those who are honest about it. Stealing a pack of gum when you were twelve years old doesn't make you a bad person or an undesirable employee.

The goal of this procedure is not to determine what the

person is guilty of, but rather if he or she is honest about it. At least then you can deal with the situation with trust. Let's say that Martha's teenage son, who has been away from home and living on the streets for the past two years, wants to come home. Knowing that her son is addicted to cocaine, she is worried about whether he can actually clean up his act. She could tell him that he can move back in only if he enrolls in a drug rehabilitation program. He will probably agree to this, whether he plans to do it or not. If he's sincere he'll say yes, and if he's lying he will also agree to her terms. This does not give Martha a true indication of her son's intentions. But Martha has read this book and instead tells her son that he can move back in if he quits cold turkey— never doing another drug whatsoever. Her son's answer will reveal his commitment to getting well, which is the real concern. Obviously her son can hardly get rid of his addiction instantly. So if he indicates that he can, she knows that he's lying about his intention to get well. However, if he says that he can't but will make strides toward getting better, she will know that he is sincere in his pursuit of wellness.

Quick Tip: People generally need a reason to lie. If there's no reason— no motivation—then you'll likely get the truth. Therefore, you want to ask for the truth before he has a reason to lie to you. Your greatest leverage always comes from knowing what kind of person you're dealing with. The time to ask the salesman about the quality of the product is not *after* you tell him that you're interested in buying it. Why? Because he may feel that it's in his best interest to lie to you. However, had you asked him this—casually, of course—before you expressed an interest, there's no real incentive for him not to tell the truth.

When you seek to gauge a person's honesty and commitment, propose a solution that you know is too difficult. If he acknowledges the difficulty of your solution, he is earnest in his desire to reach the specific objective or outcome. If he readily agrees to it, he has ulterior motives and is not being truthful.

5

ADVANCED TECHNIQUES
FOR GETTING THE TRUTH

"Enough white lies add up to manipulation."
—DAVID J. LIEBERMAN

This section offers the most advanced techniques for getting at the truth. Using a blend of hypnosis and a system I developed called Trance-Scripts, you'll be able to give commands directly to a person's unconscious mind—in conversation and without their awareness. Through this process you will be able to persuade others to tell the truth with maximum effectiveness. These techniques are extraordinary, so use them with judgment and caution!

EMBEDDED COMMANDS

This technique is used to implant suggestions directly into the unconscious. Embedded commands are just that—commands embedded in a sentence.

These can be used in conjunction with both the attack sequences and the silver bullets. To illustrate, the embedded commands are italicized in the sentence below.

If you want to *tell the truth* or not *tell the truth*, that's entirely up to you.

This sentence is received by the conscious mind in its entirety. The command—tell the truth—goes directly to the unconscious. This technique is very simple and has only two criteria. First, for maximum effectiveness the command should start with an action verb, because you're telling the mind to do something. Second, the entire command should be separated from the rest of the sentence using what is called an analog marker. You set the command portion off by one of the following: (1) Lower or raise the volume of your voice slightly while speaking the command. (2) Insert a short pause right before and then right after the command. For instance, "Sometimes we just . . . become fascinated . . . with what we're reading." (3) Gesturing with your hand while you are giving the command momentarily distracts the conscious mind, and the embedded statement is received by the unconscious mind as a command. You don't want a flagrant gesture or too long a pause. This will only confuse the person and make him question what you're doing. The objective is to be casual and relaxed.

The following is a generic example of how these would be used. The embedded commands are in italics.

I don't want you to *tell me* unless you want to. Now if you *think to yourself* on the inside *I want to tell you*, then just *say it*. When you *realize this is the right decision* you'll *tell me the truth* anyway. So we might as well *clear the air now*.

4·3·2·1

This technique is phenomenal. It works because when the brain receives several messages that it registers as truthful, then it expects what follows—the suggestion—to be truthful. As long as the suggestion is not blatantly false, the brain will accept it as true.

The process is simple. You make four truthful statements

followed by one suggestion, then three truthful statements followed by two suggestions, then two truthful statement followed by three suggestions, and finally, one truthful statement followed by four suggestions. The truthful statements can be about anything—the room you're in, the weather, anything that the brain can't argue with. The suggestions should be about what you want him or her to do. By integrating externally verifiable statements with a specific suggestion, you're leading your subject to accept your suggestion.

Scenario

A police detective is seeking a confession from a suspect. The underscored phrases are the truthful statements and the italicized words are the suggestions. You can also combine this technique with embedded commands, which are set off in parentheses.

As you're sitting in the chair, wondering what you should do, you're probably weighing your options. You want to do what's best for you and that would be to (*tell me what happened*).

We know about your past arrest for robbery. And that you got off with probation. I know that you're probably scared and *I want you to (know I'm on your side)* and *I want you to (see the benefits of telling the truth)*.

Look, you want to get out of here. And you know that I don't have the time to sit with you all day. *Getting this off your chest may make you feel better. You'll be saving yourself a lot of heartache* and *you'll be able to (get on with your life when this thing is over)*.

I know you've been around the street most of your life. *This is your chance for a fresh start. (Think about the possibilities) for yourself if you were to (go straight). You'll be able to (get a respectable job) and (take better care of your family).*

UNCONSCIOUS CREATIONS

This technique uses embedded commands in an entirely new way. You will be able to give a suggestion that creates a perceivable action so you can observe the signs of deceit without continuing to question him. Watch for the behaviors that you embed in the sentences. They will usually occur at some point during your conversation.

Examples

"I'm not saying that you should *stiffen up your body if you're lying.*"

"I don't know if you're lying. Unless you *feel like blinking your eyes fast if you are.*"

"If you . . . *like what you're reading* . . . you may . . . *smile* . . . *now.*"

With this technique, you're embedding a command that you can readily observe. Offer as many as you want. Just be sure to follow the same procedure as with the embedded commands.

DISASSOCIATION

This process helps the person become more comfortable with telling the truth. It works by dividing him into two separate people. No, not with a chain saw! You're actually dividing the psyche—setting two parts of the person against each other.

It's the old person who would lie versus the new person who would never hurt you. This process greatly alleviates the person's guilt because he no longer feels obligated to justify the actions that his "old self" was responsible for. The process of disassociation is used with great success to treat phobias.

In your conversation, continue to repeat phrases like the ones below. Make sure that they contrast the old him and the new him.

> *"Perhaps the old you was capable of this. But I know you would never do that now."*
>
> *"You're a different person than you used to be. I'm sure that you're even more upset with the old you than I am. But you're not that person anymore."*
>
> *"You're only responsible for who you are today. You are someone who is honest and trustworthy."*

These simple phrases begin to wear down his defenses. Sometimes they will work right away; other times it may take a little while. But if he keeps hearing such phrases over and over again he will break, and you will get the truth.

EYE-ACCESSING CUES

This technique works on the following principle. When a person thinks, he accesses different parts of his brain depending upon the information that is being accessed. This process can be observed by watching his eyes.

For right-handed people visual memories are accessed by the eyes going up and to the left. For a left-handed person, it's the reverse: the eyes go up and to the right. When a right-handed person seeks to *create* an image or fact, his eyes go up and to the right. And the reverse is true for the left-handed person.

Why don't you try this? Do you recall what color your first car was? If you had to think about it, there's a good chance that if you're right-handed, your eyes went up and to the left. Your eyes went up and the right if you're left-handed.

When a certain government official testified before Congress, his eyes went up and to the left each and every time he was recalling information—clearly a sign that he was relaying the facts as he remembered them, not fabricating any stories. I thought this until I happened to see a picture of him in *Time* magazine, holding a pen in his *left* hand.

You can use this technique in any conversation to determine if the person is *creating* or *recalling* information. Simply watch his eyes and you'll know whether he's recalling an event that's already occurred or making up a story about something that has never happened.

ANCHORING THE TRUTH

Do you recall Pavlov's famous dogs? During his experiments, he would put food powder in a dog's mouth and measure the drops of saliva produced as a result by way of a tube surgically inserted into the dog's mouth. But during the course of his work, Pavlov noticed that the dogs began to salivate when he merely walked into the room. This salivation could not be a reflex since it did not occur the first few times Pavlov walked in; it occurred only when the dog had learned that Pavlov's appearance signaled food. That is, Pavlov's appearance become associated with a future event: food. He called this a psychic reflex or a conditioned reflex. It has come to be called, through mistranslation, a conditioned response.

We can see examples of conditioned reflexes in our own lives. Perhaps the smell of vodka makes you sick because you had a bad experience with it several years ago. Or a certain song comes on the radio and you recall a friend you haven't thought about in years. These are all anchors. An anchor is an association between a specific set of feelings or an emotional state and some unique stimulus—an image, sound, name, taste.

We're going to use the same principle but employ it in an entirely new way. In poker there's something called a tell. That's when another player makes an unconscious gesture during a specific situation. Whenever he's nervous, for example, he may blink, look down, or move in a certain way.

Professional card players learn to pick up on these tells, providing them with an insight into the person's hand.

What you're going to do is to install a truth tell in others so you'll know when they're lying in any instance—now or in the future.

Here's how it's done. Ask a series of questions that the person can answer truthfully and easily. When he answers, anchor it with a specific movement. Then when you ask a question you don't know the answer to, fire off your truth anchor as you ask the question. He'll unconsciously feel compelled to be truthful just as Pavlov's dogs knew it was time to eat when Pavlov entered the room.

You don't want to be obvious in your choice of anchors or in your choice of questions. Make sure the questions you ask will be answered truthfully. And the anchor should not be so common that it will become diluted by inadvertent use. The questions don't have to be asked all at once, and there is no set number of questions you need to anchor.

For example, while your husband is eating his favorite food, you might ask, "Are you enjoying your dinner?" Fire off the anchor as you ask the question; you might tilt your head slightly to one side or touch your hand to your nose. Then ask a series of questions—maybe four or five—while continuing to fire off the same anchor every time you ask your question. Every so often reinforce the anchor by doing this process—a question/anchor sequence. The learned response will soon be so ingrained that any time you want the truth in response to a question, just ask your question and fire the anchor.

HEAVEN AND HELL

This technique should be used as a last resort. It is with high hope and expectation that this and all of the other processes be practiced with judgment, common sense, and decency.

Hypnosis can be used to treat phobias, anxiety disorders, and panic attacks. This technique reverses the process to instill a phobia in which dishonesty creates overwhelming anxiety. If pain is linked to deceit and pleasure to the truth, confessing becomes the only way to reduce the pain.

We use a process similar to anchoring the truth, except whenever something painful or negative happens to this person—he bangs his foot, he gets into argument with a neighbor—you anchor it. Whenever he feels disappointed or becomes upset, anchor it. Then ask your question and if it's not the response you want—if you feel he's lying—fire off the pain anchor. He'll quickly associate lying to you with pain. The only way to alleviate this pain will be to tell the truth. To further increase the association, contrast it by using a different anchor linked to pleasant experiences—sexual arousal, eating, relaxing, etc.

THE BRIDGE

In part 2 we touched briefly on the importance of rapport. When we are in synch with another person our communication flows effortlessly. When we consciously seek to get in rapport with someone—to align ourselves psychologically—we align ourselves physically. Examples of this are matching a person's gestures, posture, or rate of speech. This is called pacing. Once you've done this, you switch to what's called leading. This can be extremely effective when done in the following way:

After establishing rapport with the other person, you feed him everything that he may be thinking about the conversation. These statements accurately reflect his thinking. This aligns you psychologically. Then you lead his *thinking* by explaining why the truth is the best route for him to take. And if this process is done right, he will follow.

Example

"I know that you think you're not ready to tell me the truth. I'm sure that you wish this entire conversation wasn't taking place right now, and that it could just be over with. I'm sure that you think I'm going to be upset with you and that we're going to get into a fight over it. You may be thinking that there's no reason to tell me. Maybe I'm making a bigger deal out of it than it really warrants. I understand. We all make mistakes, and this is one that you wish would just go away. I'm sure I would feel exactly as you do if I were in your position. But since I'm not, *I can only tell you what it feel like to be in mine*. [This phrase begins the lead.]

"It's all okay. It really is. Let's have an honest discussion. You tell me exactly what happened and you'll know that it's the right thing to do. I'd be happy, and I know you will too, to be able to put this behind us. That we can move on. Let's do that because it makes sense for both of us."

ADVANCED CONVERSATION STOPPERS: TRANCE PHRASES

These conversation stoppers use phrases that are mild trance inducers. In other words, they cause the listener to zone out temporarily while his brain tries to process the information. Use them when you need to gain control of the conversation or to regroup. They give you some time to collect your thoughts while others lose their train of thought. You may have to read them several times yourself because of the "huh" effect.

1. "Why are you asking me what you don't know for sure?"
2. "Do you really believe what you thought you knew?"
3. "Could you give me . . . an example . . . would be helpful."
4. "You can pretend anything and master it."
5. "I understand what you're . . . saying . . . it doesn't make it true."
6. "If you expected me to believe that, you wouldn't have said it."
7. "Your question is what you knew it would be, isn't it?"
8. "Your response says what you're unaware of."
9. "Do you believe that you knew what you thought?"
10. "How do you stop a thought once you get it?"

11. "Why would you believe something that's not true?"
12. "Why are you agreeing with what you already know?"
13. "What happens when you get a thought?"
14. "The less you try the more you'll agree . . ."
15. "Are you unaware of what you forgot?"

SEE FOR YOURSELF

The power of expectation and suggestion can be used with tremendous results. While you could be relentless in your pursuit to get the truth from someone, his mind may be ready to defend the assault. But when his own mind turns against itself, he will do the work for you.

Have you ever noticed what happens when you buy a new car? Suddenly it seems like everyone on the road is driving that same car. Or if you're on a diet, everywhere you turn is a bakery or ice-cream store. Reality has not changed, only your perception of it has. When you can't change someone's reality to get to the truth, alter how he sees it instead. This can be just as effective.

If you were to tell a neighbor that there has been a rash of break-ins in the neighborhood, over the next few days she'll notice the garbage cans seem out of order; the mailbox looks "funny"; the car across the street looks suspicious. At night, she'll hear every creek and noise in the house. Maybe she's heard them a thousand times before, but now she's listening to them. Now they may mean something.

The key to using this technique is to implant an artificial

suggestion and let it manifest inside the person's mind. This technique gets the person to rethink her behavior with or without your confronting her directly. Please note that this technique may induce a temporary state of mild paranoia, especially if two or more people make the same suggestion.

Scenario

You think that a coworker has been stealing office supplies.

Sample question formation I: "Samantha, have you noticed that people seem to be looking at you a little funny?" You can be sure Samantha will "see" everyone looking at her, and it will consume her attention until she stops.

Sample question formation II: "Samantha, I think the whole office knows about the office supplies—have you ever noticed how they stare at you sometimes?" This formation is more direct and confrontational.

You'll notice that if Samantha is in fact stealing office supplies, she will soon believe that everyone is "on to her" because she will see everyone staring at her.

6

PSYCHOLOGY ON YOUR SIDE

"Men stumble over the truth from time to time, but most
pick themselves up and hurry off
as if nothing has happened."
—WINSTON CHURCHILL

In order to get to the truth you need to know how to take control of a situation, command authority, and above all, predict someone else's response. These ten commandments of human behavior will help you to navigate the sometimes turbulent waters of conversation and her twin sister, debate. By understanding how the brain processes information, you will be able to easily influence anyone to tell the truth.

TEN COMMANDMENTS OF HUMAN BEHAVIOR

1. Ninety percent of the decisions we make are based on emotion. We then use logic to justify our actions. If you appeal to someone on a strictly logical basis, you will have little chance of persuading him. If you're not getting the truth, phrases such as "Honesty is the best policy" or "Lies just hurt everyone" won't sway anybody. You need to translate logic and sensible thinking into an emotion-based statement—and give direct benefits for that person to come clean.

For instance, a mother speaking to her child might try, "When you lie, it hurts me. I want to be able to trust you. Trusting you means that you'll have more responsibility—you'll be able to do more fun things like have sleepovers and go to the petting zoo with your friends."

You should offer specific benefits that appeal to the person's emotions. The attack sequences and silver bullets are all emotionally charged.

2. How we deal with good and bad news depends on how it is internalized. When a person becomes unusually depressed about an event in her life, it's often because of three mental distortions: (1) she feels that the situation is permanent; (2) she feels that it is critical, meaning that it's more significant than it really is; and (3) that it is all-consuming, that it will invade and pervade other areas of her life. When any or all of these beliefs are present and elevated, it will dramatically increase her anxiety and despondency.

Conversely, when we think of a problem as temporary, isolated, and insignificant, it doesn't concern us at all. By artificially inflating or deflating these factors in the mind of another, you can instantly alter their attitude toward any situation, be it positive or negative.

3. When a person becomes adamant about his position, change the one thing that you can—his physiology. A person's emotional state is directly related to his physical state. If he gets locked into a position of denial or refusal, get him to move his body. This prevents what is called mind-lock and makes it easier for him to change his psychological position. If he's sitting down, have him get up and walk around the room. If he's standing, try to get him to sit down. When our body is in a fixed position, our mind can become similarly frozen.

4. Don't ask someone to change his mind without giving him additional information. Remember that while you're talking to the person he listens with his ego—and you must accommodate it. Many people see changing their mind as a sign of weakness. He's given up and you've won.

So instead of asking him to change his mind, allow him to make a new decision based on additional information. Politicians have a penchant for this because they never want to appear wishy-washy. They rarely say that they've changed their mind on an issue—rather, they say their "position has evolved," as it were.

For example, you might say, "I can see why you said that then, but in light of the fact that [a new bit of information to justify him changing his mind], I think you owe me an explanation."

However, the way in which this new information is introduced is crucial. The more recent the information is, or appears to be, the more effective you will be. If you bring up a fact that occurred some time ago, a fact that he was simply unaware of, he may not want to look foolish for not having known about it. Therefore the more timely the information, the more comfortable he will feel in reevaluating his thinking.

5. Sometimes you need to amplify the problem in order to reach a solution. Some time ago I was over at a friend's house when his six-year-old announced that he was angry because he couldn't have ice cream for breakfast. With my friends' consent, I said the following to his son: "You're

right, Stuart, you are too upset to do anything but be angry. You'll probably need to sit there for two whole hours until it passes." Needless to say, Stuart got over his anger fast.

A friend of mine had a secretary who was constantly straightening up his office. He would ask her not to, but she insisted that it should be kept clean and organized. She had been with him for over fifteen years and he wasn't about to dismiss her over this. Nonetheless, this habit became very annoying. The solution? He went out of his way to make a mess. Every morning the office looked like a disaster area. Finally his secretary mentioned that she thought he was taking advantage of her good nature by being such a slob. She stopped tidying up soon afterward.

When arguing becomes futile, stop. Go the other direction, reversing your position entirely. Give the other person an exaggerated version of what he wants. This will often cause him to retreat to more neutral ground.

6. People do what you expect them to do. If you say something ten times, you clearly don't expect them to listen to you. Notice the way people in authority—police, for example—take control of a situation. They don't scream, yell, or carry on. A wave of their hand, and the traffic stops. They say things once, and directly.

If you're taken to the hospital with a broken leg, the doctor tells you what needs to be done. You aren't given options. There's no deliberation or argument, and you're not asked for your opinion. If you're told that you need x-rays and a cast, then you get x-rays and a cast. Could you imagine if your doctor said, "You know, I think your leg is broken. What do you think?" You expect him to tell you what the situation is and what needs to be done.

Do the same in conversation. When you give an order, expect people to follow it and they will. When you shout, you send the message "I'm shouting so you'll listen to me." The best way to get a person's attention is to speak softly and directly.

Not only will people often do what you expect them to do, but they often feel how you suggest they should feel. Take a look at three distinct examples of this influence at work in our everyday life.

A. When a small child falls, if his parent makes a big deal out of it, he will likely cry and become more upset. The child's thoughts are, "Mom knows best, and if she thinks I hurt myself I must have."

B. The well-known placebo effect can induce physiological changes such as lowering blood pressure or controlling cholesterol levels. With no more than a sugar pill, a patient's body may react as if it were given the actual medication.

C. Someone says you look tired and your whole disposition changes. Try this on a coworker and you'll notice a complete change of body language. If you want to be nice, try the converse and tell someone she looks great. Watch a smile appear and her eyes widen. While she may deny the compliment, watch her face to she how she really feels about it.

7. When we ask a favor of someone, common sense dictates that we might want that person to be in a good mood.

The thinking is, if he's relaxed and feeling good he's more likely to give us what we ask for. This is usually true, but it doesn't always work when you ask for the truth. When you want someone to come clean with the facts, you're asking for more than a favor. You have to assume that it—the truth—is something that he doesn't want to give. Thus the more comfortable things are, the less his incentive is. The best time to seek your confession is when he's tired, hungry, thirsty, whatever. He won't be thinking clearly and will be looking to end the conversation as soon as possible. Of course he's going to be more agitated and grumpy. Nonetheless, if the only way he can become more comfortable is to tell you what you want, then he will.

8. You must be able to walk away. If your opponent senses desperation, you're sunk. You're only as strong as your alternatives, and the more attractive your alternatives, the more power you have. When you're desperate, the facts look grossly out of proportion. When this happens, you'll be apt to do what you never should do: make a decision out of fear. When your options are limited, your perspective is distorted; your thinking is emotional, not logical. This is true for all of us. If you perceive your power to be nonexistent you are likely to give in without good cause. By increasing your alternatives and narrowing the other person's options, you gain considerable leverage. The equation that determines the balance of leverage is simple. It comes down to who needs who more. There's a saying that the person who cares less, wins. One way to increase your power is to demonstrate that what your opponent has to offer—in this

case, the truth—can be obtained through other means—in this case, other people. This decreases his power, and hence his leverage.

9. It's important to know how human beings process information. When it comes to doing what we like, we do what's called *single-tasking*. When we think about things we don't want to do, we do what's called *multitasking*. What does this all mean? Well, if you have to pay your bills but never feel like doing it, what's the thought process you might go through? You think, *I've got to get all of the bills together* and *organize them into different piles; get out my checkbook, stamps, and envelopes; address each letter; write out the check; balance the checkbook;* and so on. When it comes to doing something you enjoy doing, you internalize the steps in larger groups. For example, if you enjoy cooking, the steps might be, go the store and come home and make dinner. If you hated to cook, everything from waiting on line at the supermarket to cleaning the dishes afterwards would enter into the equation.

Fine, but what's the practical use of this? Well, if you want to give someone a motive to do something, you're going to show him that it's simple and easy. If you want to discourage a behavior, you need only stretch out the number of steps into a long, boring, and arduous process. Same event, but depending upon how it's internalized, you'll generate a completely different feeling toward it.

10. Every action human beings take is motivated either out of a need to avoid pain or the desire to gain pleasure—or

a combination of the two. What you link pleasure and pain to determines how a person will respond.

If you want to influence a person's behavior, you need to attach pain to the direction you don't want him to move in and pleasure to the direction you want him to move toward. Too often out of anger or ignorance we lose sight of this powerful motivating tool. If someone's not being truthful with you, do you want to shout, "You're a no-good liar! I knew you'd only cause me misery. Tell me the damn truth and then get the hell out of my life!" This is not an effective strategy. It's a simple equation: if the benefit of being truthful outweighs the benefit of lying, you will get the truth. However, a crucial criterion needs to be met. The benefit should provide for an easy out. This is something that most people don't take into consideration. The liar above all else wants to change the conversation, move on, and put this behind him. When you outline the benefits make sure to include, if you can, that the subject will never again be brought up, it will be forgotten about, and you both will be able to put this in the past. You could offer him the greatest incentive for being truthful, but if he thinks a lengthy conversation and constant reminders will follow, he's not going to budge. The silver bullets are good examples of how to phrase your request for the truth using the pleasure/pain principle.

7

INTERNAL TRUTH BLOCKERS: WE LIE LOUDEST WHEN WE LIE TO OURSELVES

"Once he finds out who he is, what can console him?
. . . for on Earth
Everyone who lives, lives in a dream."
—CALDERÓN DE LA BARCA

You have all the tools necessary to spot deceit and to ferret out the truth. However, several factors can interfere with and even completely block your ability to detect deceit. The good news is that being aware of these factors neutralizes their power and leaves you free to examine the facts as they are.

SELF-DECEPTION

The easiest person to lie to is someone who wants to be deceived. While several factors can get in the way of our getting to the truth, the worst offenders are usually ourselves. If you don't want to see the truth, you often will not. We all have a friend whose boyfriend comes home late every night from work. He's seen around town with women half his age, smells like perfume, and is constantly taking business trips on the weekend. Yet despite all of the evidence she refuses to see the truth. She accepts him at his word, and that is that.

When we don't want to see the truth we'll lie to ourselves. These lies are the toughest to spot because they are our own. There's no objectivity to give us perspective.

People spend millions calling 900 numbers to hear a recording of their lucky lottery numbers. We would like to believe that we could make a thousand dollars an hour in our spare time working at home from the kitchen table. Our desire to believe strongly influences what we see as our reality, from miracle wrinkle creams to guaranteed weight-loss pills. And our desire *not to see* filters out vital information that would often give us clues to discovering the truth.

Only the exceptional person is willing to look at what he doesn't want to see, listen to what he doesn't want to hear, and believe that which he wishes would not exist.

When you go into a meeting wanting it to work out, you'll overlook too many things that may make it a bad deal. You must try to remain as objective as possible—as if you were reviewing the information for someone else. Wishful thinking, desire, and hope cannot allow you to lose sight of reality.

The secret lies in learning how to suspend your interests. And yes, there is an easy way to do this usually difficult task. Watch out for the three Cs. They are compliments, confirmation, and confrontation. If you're listening with any of these preconceptions in mind, the information is likely to be distorted. In other words, if you're looking for praise, looking to confirm that which you already know, or looking for an argument, you will miss the true meaning behind the message.

OPINIONS, ATTITUDES, AND BELIEFS

In the previous paragraphs, we saw how our desire to see or not to see colors our perception of reality. What we *believe* to be true also distorts our perception. All of our prejudices, beliefs, attitudes, and opinions filter out the truth.

If you grew up to respect and revere authority and were taught never to question an authority figure, this belief will greatly inhibit your ability to be objective about information that comes from someone in such a position. Similarly, if you believe that all salesmen are thieves or that all police are corrupt, it becomes impossible to see what is there. Instead you see a projection of your own ideals, beliefs, and prejudices.

Sometimes we need to generalize about our world; with literally thousands of decisions to make each day, we can't look at everything as if we were seeing it for first time. There are times, however, when it's vitally important to suspend your beliefs. Then and only then can you see things as they are, not how you believe them to be.

DON'T LET YOUR EMOTIONS GET THE BETTER OF YOU

Strong emotions cloud our perception of reality. Over two thousand years ago, Aristotle had this to say about emotion and distortion: "Under the influence of strong feeling we are easily deceived. The coward under the influence of fear and the lover under that of love have such illusions that the coward owing to a trifling resemblance thinks he sees an enemy and the lover his beloved."

Emotional states are either self-induced, externally

brought on, or arise from a combination of the two. Some of the more powerful ones are: guilt, intimidation, appeal to ego, fear, curiosity, our desire to be liked, and love. If you're operating in any of these states, your judgment is likely to be impaired. Furthermore, anyone who uses any of these is attempting to move you from logic to emotion—to a playing field that's not so level. In the process the truth gets lost because you're not operating logically and can't effectively see the evidence before you, let alone weigh it. Some generic examples of how these manipulations sound are as follows:

Guilt: "How can you even say that? I'm hurt that you wouldn't trust me. I just don't know who you are anymore."

Fear: "You know, you might just lose this entire deal. I don't think that's going to make your boss very happy. I sure hope you know what you're doing. I'm telling you that you won't get a better deal anywhere else. You're a fool if you think otherwise."

Appeal to ego: "I can see that you're a smart person. I wouldn't try to put anything past you. How could I? You'd be on to me in a second."

Curiosity: "Look, you only live once. Try it. You can always go back to how things were before. It might be fun, exciting—a real adventure."

Desire to be liked: "I thought you were a real player. So did everybody else. This is going to be a real disappointment if you don't come through for us."

Love: "If you loved me you wouldn't question me. Of course I have only your best interest at heart. I wouldn't lie to you. You know that deep down inside, don't you?"

Look and listen objectively—not only at the words but

at the message. These internal truth blockers interfere with your ability to digest the facts. When these emotions creep into your thinking, temporarily suspend your feelings and look in front of you, not inside yourself.

EXTERNAL TRUTH BLOCKERS: TRICKS OF THE TRADE

"The truth is the same from every angle. A lie always
needs to be facing forward."
—DAVID J. LIEBERMAN

Unlike internal truth blockers, which we bring on ourselves, these truth blockers are done to us. These are the psychological secrets of the experts, the tricks of the trade—factors that can affect your judgment in objectively evaluating information.

No matter what area of life we're in, we're always selling something. In business you're selling a product or service. In your personal life you're selling yourself and your ideas. Regardless of the situation, the reason you don't succeed is always going to be the same: the person doesn't believe what you're saying is true.

Let's say you're a real estate broker. Someone who is not investing with you may say "I have to think about it" or "I have to talk to my wife." But really it all comes down to one thing. If your prospect believed what you were saying was true—that you would make him money—then he would invest with you, wouldn't he? Establishing credibility is the key to influencing the behavior of others. When credibility can't be gained through the facts, distortion of the truth is what often follows.

These techniques can be difficult to escape because they're based on psychological principles of human nature. The good news is that these tactics are a lot like a magic trick. Once you know how the trick is done, you can't be fooled.

Wow! You're Just Like Me

We all tend to like, trust, and subsequently be influenced by people like ourselves. We feel a sense of connection and understanding. If you've been to a casino recently, you may have noticed something interesting on every employee's name tag. It looks a lot like this:

Jim Smith
V. P., Marketing
Atlanta, GA

The employee's hometown is right on the tag. Why? Because it helps to create a bond with anyone who has lived there or maybe has a relative in that area. It invariably starts a conversation and the gambler begins to feel connected with this person. Something as innocuous as a name tag has created instant rapport and possibly a loyal customer.

You may be thinking that this seems harmless enough, and you'd be right. What's the big deal, anyway? Well, if all that was affected by this psychological trait was name tags, then we wouldn't have to worry. But it's not. It's much more pervasive and far-reaching than you could ever imagine.

Listing all the situations in which this rule could be used on you would fill a book on its own. Therefore, here are the three most popular ways that it infiltrates our lives.

1. Watch out when you're asked about your hobbies, hometown, values, favorite foods, etc., only to be followed with the obligatory "Me too, what a coincidence."

2. Another aspect of this rule is that if someone is nice to us, we not only like him more but are more likely to agree with him. Don't you know this to be true in your own life? If he's agreeing to everything you say, whether or not it makes sense, watch out. The phrase "flattery will get you nowhere" couldn't be further from the truth.

A great little fable by Aesop illustrates this nicely. It's called "The Fox and the Crow."

A fox spied a crow sitting on a branch of a tall tree with a golden piece of cheese in her beak. The fox, who was both clever and hungry, quickly thought of a plan to get the cheese away from the crow.

Pretending to notice the crow for the first time, the fox exclaimed, "My, what a beautiful bird! I must say that is the most elegant black plumage I have ever seen. Look how it shines in the sun. Simply magnificent!"

The crow was flattered by all this talk about her feathers. She listened to every sugary word that the fox spoke. The fox continued: "I must say that this is the most beautiful bird in the world. But I wonder, can such a stunning bird have an equally splendid voice? That," said the cunning fox, "would be too much to ask." The crow, believing the fox's words, opened her beak to let out an ear-piercing *caw*! As she did so, the cheese tumbled out of her mouth and was gobbled up instantly by the fox. The moral: never trust a flatterer.

Does this mean that you should be wary of every single compliment and always assume the one who compliments you has an ulterior motive? Of course not. Just be alert to praise that drips with insincerity.

3. Finally, remember our discussion about rapport in part 2? Well, it can just as easily be used on you. Rapport creates trust. It allows the other to build a psychological bridge to you. You feel more comfortable and your gullibility increases. Take note if your movements, rate of speech, or tone are echoed by another.

Beware the Stranger Bearing Gifts

Ever wonder why religious groups offer a flower or some other gift in the airport? They know that most people will feel compelled to give them a small donation. We know we don't have to, but we can become uncomfortable, even though we didn't ask for the gift in the first place.

When someone gives us something, we often feel indebted to him. When you are presented with a request, make sure that you're not acting out of a sense of obligation. This rule can take many forms—it's not limited to gifts. You could be offered information, a concession, or even someone's time. Don't think that salespeople don't know that if they invest a lot of time with you, showing you a product, demonstrating how it works, you will feel somewhat obligated to buy it, even if you're not sure that you really want it. The key is to decide what's right independent of the other person's interest in your decision.

It's Half Price! But Half of What?

This principle states that facts are likely to be interpreted differently based upon the order in which they're presented. In other words, we compare and contrast. In an electronics store the salesperson might show you accessories to go with your stereo system *after* you've agreed to buy it. Somehow the fifty-dollar carrying case and a thirty-dollar warranty doesn't seem that much in the wake of an eight-hundred-dollar system. Because he has shown you the costlier items first, your perspective shifts and the items seen afterwards are deemed more reasonable.

A less-than-reputable used car salesman might show you several cars that are priced 20 to 30 percent higher than they should be. Then he'll show you a car that's priced fairly and you'll think it's a great deal. To you, it feels as if you're getting more car for the money—what a bargain! When really you only think that because you're comparing it to the other cars.

Other examples of this principle are price markdowns. An item that's been reduced from $500 to $200 certainly seems like a better bargain than something that sells for $150. The contrast on the sale item makes it more attractive, even if it's not as nice as the item that sells for less. "I know it's expensive, but look at what it used to sell for" is the familiar retort.

In some of the finer restaurants, guests are treated to sorbet between courses. This is done to clear the palate. Flavors from previous dishes won't mix with others, so that each dish may be enjoyed completely. When you have a decision to make, why not clear your mental palate? To do this you need only consider each decision by itself. This can best be accomplished by letting time pass between decisions and by independently determining the value of the object.

Just Do This One Little Thing for Me?

Know when to stick to your guns and when not to. Most of us have a strong tendency to act in a manner consistent with our previous actions—even if it's not a good idea. It's just human nature. We are compelled to be consistent in our words, thought, beliefs, and actions.

It has to do with the ability to make a decision independent of previous decisions. And the higher a person's self-esteem, the greater the chance that he or she will make independent decisions. The following, which is from my book *Instant Analysis*, deals with this phenomenon. If you have a low or negative self-image, then you feel more compelled to justify your previous actions so you can be "right." You will eat food that you don't want because you ordered it. You will watch a video that you really don't want to see because you went "all the way to the video store in the rain to get it." You continually try to "make things right," justifying old actions with consistent behavior. In other words, watching the video that you went to get makes getting the video the smart thing to do, even if you no longer feel like watching it. Your primary concern is with being right, even if it means compromising present judgment in order to satisfy and justify past behaviors. This is done in the hope that you can turn things around so that you can be right.

The ultimate example of this behavior is the process of cult recruiting. You may wonder how an intelligent and aware person could ever get involved in a cult—where the members give up family, friends, possessions, and in some very sad instances, their lives. The higher a person's self-esteem, the less likely he or she will be to fall prey to a cult—primarily because a person with a positive self-image can admit to himself, and to others, that he's done something stupid. Those who lack self-worth cannot afford to question their judgment, worth, or intelligence. The method employed in cult recruitment is to involve the person slowly over a period of time. Each new step of involvement forces the person to justify his or her previous behavior. This is why cultists don't just walk up to someone and say, "Hey, do you want to join our cult and give up all of your possessions?"

This rule can greatly influence your decision-making process. Essentially, by getting you to agree to small, seemingly innocuous requests, the person sets you up for something larger. By agreeing to the small requests, you justify your behavior by realigning your thinking as follows: "I must really care about this person or I wouldn't be helping him" and "I must really care about this cause or I wouldn't be doing any of this."

To avoid others using this rule on you, beware if you are asked to commit to something, even in a small way. This request is usually followed by a slightly greater request, and over time your sense of commitment is built up to the point where you feel locked into your decision.

When you make decisions, notice if your best interests are being served or if you're simply trying to "make right" a previous behavior.

The Bandwagon Effect

This principle states that we have a tendency to see an action as appropriate if other people are doing it. This psychological trait invades many areas of our life. Laugh tracks for television comedy shows come courtesy of this principle as well. Do we think that something is funnier if others are laughing? Absolutely. Your neighbor, whom you never looked at twice, suddenly appears more attractive when you're told that every woman is dying to date him. Cherry red—the color that the car salesman told you is the hottest seller of the season—suddenly becomes a must-have. The key to avoiding the influence of this rule is to separate your level of interest from other people's desire. Just because you're told that something is the latest, best, hottest, or biggest seller doesn't make it right for you.

A White Lab Coat Doesn't Make Anyone an Expert

Of all the psychological tools, this is by far the most used and abused by retailers. We all remain to some degree quite susceptible to our earlier conditioning regarding authority—mainly, it is to be respected. This is fine, except that the abuses of our vulnerability are flagrant and rampant. Have you ever noticed what cosmetic salespeople in department stores wear? Lab coats! Does this not seem odd? Why do they wear them? Because it makes them look like experts. And we are more likely to believe what they have to say because they are perceived as more credible.

Recently my friend had told me that he had rented the absolute worst movie he had ever seen in his life. When I asked what possessed him to rent it, he replied, "The guy behind the counter told me I would like it." As soon as he said this, he realized how silly he had been. What on earth does the guy behind the counter know about my friend or his taste in movies? Just because someone's behind a counter, wearing a lab coat, or holding a clipboard, that doesn't make him an expert.

Rare Doesn't Always Mean Valuable

This principle states that the harder something is to acquire, the greater the value we place on its attainment. In essence, we want what we can't have and want what is hard to obtain even more.

"We're probably out of stock on that item. It's a huge seller. But if I did have one available, you would want it, right?" There's a better chance you would say yes when the possibility of attainment is at its lowest.

Compare the above sentence with the following one and see if you would be as apt to agree to the purchase: "We have a warehouse full of them. Should I write up the order now?" The impetus to act just isn't there this time. No urgency, no scarcity, and no desire. The key to avoid this rule being used on you is to ask yourself this question: would I still want it if there were a million just like it and no one wanted any of them?

A Color Pie Chart Doesn't Make It True

Benjamin Disraeli put it best when he said, "There are three kinds of lies: lies, damned lies and statistics." It never ceases to amaze me just how easily swayed we become by something that "looks" official. Just because someone points to a color graph as "proof" doesn't make everything he's saying true. Don't be swayed by the mode of the message—rather, focus on the message itself. How many of us listen to a salesman's pitch, only to be presented with a nice color brochure outlining everything that's just been said? At what point did we come to believe that the printing press doesn't lie?

There's an old saying that goes "Nobody ever sells a horse because it's a bad horse. They sell it for tax purposes." Often we don't stop and ask ourselves, "Does this make sense?" A dash of common sense can go a long, long way.

I'm on Your Side

This technique is used to gain credibility. When it is done effectively, you would swear that you've just made a new best friend who has only your best interest at heart. For this rule, he manufactures a scenario to gain your trust, then uses this trust in a real-life situation.

For example, let's say that you're in a mattress store and considering buying the Super Deluxe—a firm, top-of-the-line bed. The salesman tells you that if you want it he'll order it for you, but he feels you should know something first. He proceeds to tell you that while the consumer would never realize it, this manufacturer sometimes uses recycled materials on the inside.

What has he accomplished by this? He has gained your complete confidence. He's risking a sale to tell you something that you'd never find out otherwise. Now you'll be inclined to trust anything he says. At this point he shows you the Supreme Deluxe. It's priced slightly higher than your first choice, but has no used materials inside.

Look at What You're Getting, Not What You're Promised

To avoid being deceived, evaluate a person's integrity based upon what is being presented, not what is promised. Henry was an older man who went store to store selling pocket watches. To those in the store, salespeople and shoppers alike, he was a peddler. And he retired a millionaire. He did nothing that was illegal per se. How did he become so wealthy selling pocket watches? Mainly because he never sold the watch. What he sold was the story.

Henry would walk into the shop and ask if anyone would like to buy a beautiful handcrafted crystal lamp. The cost was only thirty-five dollars, hundreds less than what one would expect to pay.

He made the lamps himself and enjoyed "giving them away." Since he had only one sample he would need to take orders. He diligently took down the names and addresses of each eager person and refused to accept any sort of deposit. "You'll pay when you get it and when you're happy with it," he would say, smiling. Henry had now established himself as a trusting person and one who had a beautiful product at a fantastic price. He has their trust and their confidence.

Henry also carried a large box with a handle. And invariably someone at some point would ask what was in the box. This is when Henry went to work. He opened the box, revealing beautiful sterling silver pocket watches individually wrapped and protected. He told his eager audience just about anything he wanted to about the watches. They had no reason to doubt him or their value. After all, look at everything he had "done" for them so far. Henry would sell the pocket watches to most of the nice folks who placed orders for his lamp. Nobody ever did get a lamp—just an overpriced pocket watch, sold to them by a kind old man.

Remember Henry the next time you make a decision based upon something that has been promised, but not delivered.

RULE 11

Well, Can You at Least Do This?

If you're asked to do a rather large favor for someone only to decline his request for help, beware. A smaller favor, the one he really wants you to do, may follow. We are more likely to agree to a smaller request if we're first presented with a larger one. There are three psychological motivations at work:

1. You feel that in contrast to the first request, the smaller one is no big deal.

2. You feel bad for not coming through on his original favor, and this seems like a fair compromise.

3. You don't want to be perceived as unreasonable. Refusing the large request is one thing. And this small favor is not going to kill you.

I'll Show You

Nobody wants to be prejudged or negatively evaluated. That is to say, people dislike being thought of as lesser, in any way, shape, or form. Here's how those who understand this rule can use it against you. You walk into a clothing store and ask to see a certain designer sweater. The salesman shows you where it is and adds, "It may be a little pricey for you, we have some less expensive ones over there." "I'll show that jerk," you think to yourself. "I'll buy this sweater and prove that I can afford it." You leave mad with an expensive purchase, head held high, of course. The salesman? He's smiling all the way to the bank. This rule uses what is commonly referred to as reverse psychology. By implying what he "thought" you could afford, he forced your ego to prove to him wrong.

CONCLUSION

Whether it's business or personal matters—from casual conversations to in-depth negotiations—the techniques that you have learned will significantly change the way you relate to the rest of the world. Now that you've gained that extra edge, you'll enjoy an unprecedented opportunity to use the most important secrets governing human behavior for enhancing and advancing your business and personal relationships.

There will probably never be a way to stop people from trying to lie to you, but now you'll be ready for them. And with each new encounter, in any situation, you will never be lied to again.

ADDITIONAL INFORMATION

Dr. Lieberman offers special programs, training, and workshops on a limited basis. Please send your request for information to the following contact address. All inquiries must be on official government or corporate letterhead.

For general information or to be placed on our mailing list, simply send your request to the following address.

Lieberman & Associates
PO Box 241
Greenvale, NY 11548

Visit us on the Internet at:
www.Truth123.com

19.95

158.2 L
Lieberman, David J.
Never be lied to again.